HISTORIC WALKS
IN DERBYSHIRE

HISTORIC WALKS
IN DERBYSHIRE

by
Elaine Burkinshaw

2 POLICE SQUARE, MILNTHORPE, CUMBRIA LA7 7PY
www.cicerone.co.uk

o|s Ordnance Survey® This product includes mapping data licensed from Ordnance Survey® with the permission of the Controller of Her Majesty's Stationery Office. © Crown copyright 2002. *All rights reserved.* Licence number PU100012932

ACKNOWLEDGEMENTS

I would like to thank my family for their special contributions to this book, in particular my dad, Peter Mellor, who assisted with the maps. Thanks also to husband Andrew, mum and dad for accompanying me on many of the walks and putting up with my conversations with my dictaphone.

Advice to Readers

Readers are advised that while every effort is taken by the author to ensure the accuracy of this guidebook, changes can occur which may affect the contents. It is advisable to check locally on transport, accommodation, shops, etc, but even rights of way can be altered. Paths can be affected by forestry work, landslip or changes of ownership.

The publisher would welcome notes of any such changes.

Front cover: Edensor from Chatsworth Park, Walk 24

CONTENTS

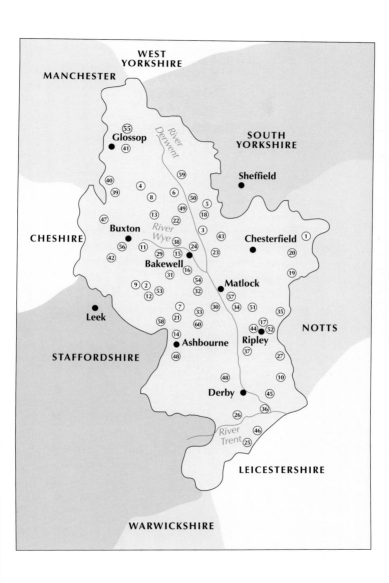

**Chatsworth,
Bakewell,
Derbyshire,**
DE45 1PP

Baslow 582204

I welcome Elaine Burkinshaw's latest book on walking, particularly as it includes Chatsworth.

Before old age overtook me I was a keen walker, and one of the few things I am proud of is having achieved the Lyke Wake Walk in a reasonably respectable time. I have only done parts of the Pennine Way, but at least have done the great climb from Edale.

I warmly recommend this new book and hope it will encourage more people to enjoy the wonderful walking in this county.

Andrew Cavendish
Duke of Devonshire
Chatsworth
Derbyshire

PREFACE

Historic Walks in Derbyshire is my third walking guide, following *Walking in Sherwood Forest and the Dukeries* (Cicerone Press) and *Discovery Walks in North East Derbyshire* (Sigma Press), which were both inspired by a desire to explore new local walks as an alternative to the Peak District, to which the majority of walkers living in Sheffield are automatically drawn. Although my husband, Andrew, and I currently live in South Yorkshire, we are only 200 metres from the Derbyshire border and very close to Nottinghamshire. Indeed, I have lived all my life in and around Sheffield and Manchester.

This search for a change led to a very pleasant surprise as I had simply not appreciated the scenic quality or historical interest sitting on my doorstep, and I wanted to share this with others and hopefully persuade them to dip their toes into fresh soil. So for several years I did not set foot in the Peak District, and I must admit I genuinely did miss it, and Andrew would often echo my thoughts. I was ready to return to some familiar favourite spots in the Peak District and to discover the hidden delights of south Derbyshire, which was virtually unknown to me.

Numerous walking books have been written on the Peak District, Britain's first and most visited national park, which covers roughly half of the county of Derbyshire. Comparatively few guides, however, provide comprehensive coverage of the whole of the county or of south Derbyshire in isolation – a part of the county that adds an extra dimension in terms of scenery and completes a number of links in chains of tourist attractions identified in this guide.

All the walks in this guide are easy to moderate in terms of the difficulty of the terrain or length, as I have avoided the more challenging geography of the Dark Peak moorlands. This is partly due to my own scenic preferences and partly because I would describe myself as a rambler rather than a serious hiker or mountaineer. In addition, this has enabled me to include with each walk various tourist attractions, to encourage families, new and infrequent walkers, and those seeking to explore more of what Derbyshire has to offer.

With this aim in mind I had little difficulty in compiling 60 walks set against the backdrop of the uniquely contrasting and outstandingly beautiful Derbyshire landscape and covering an extensive range of themes. Indeed, the problem was not what to include but what to leave out in the space permitted. For example, there are remnants of ancient civilisations, fine market towns and villages, Derbyshire customs and traditions, caverns and mines, castles, grand country houses and parklands galore, craft centres, factory shops, gardens, Georgian and Victorian spa resorts, industrial heritage and transport history, adventure and theme parks for the young and much more. All of this in the Heart of England with excellent accessibility from all parts of Britain and within an hour's drive for half the population of England.

Before I wrote this book my family and I already had a real love for the exceptional beauty of Derbyshire, but through my research our appreciation of the county has been greatly enhanced. It would give me great pleasure to share this with as many other families as possible. Happy walking.

Elaine Burkinshaw

INTRODUCTION

Without doubt Derbyshire is one of the most picturesque counties in England, renowned for its varied scenic beauty ranging from wild sombre moorland in the north to sparkling rivers laced with delightful deep dales in the central area and gentle rolling countryside further south. Derbyshire has it all, except for a coastline and natural lakes. The poet John Ruskin, whose work was heavily influenced by his many visits to the county, described it as 'a lovely child's first alphabet' because 'in its very minuteness it is the most educational of all the districts of beautiful landscapes known to me'. Another poet inspired by Derbyshire's countryside was Byron, who in a letter to the Irish poet Thomas Moore said 'there are things in Derbyshire as noble as in Switzerland or Greece'.

Derbyshire is situated at the crossroads of England where highland meets lowland. Many people tend to think of Derbyshire and the well-known Peak District (1437sq km/555sq miles, created as Britain's first national park in 1951) as virtually one and the same thing, but this is totally incorrect, as the bulk of the Peak District sits in the north of Derbyshire and overlaps into several other counties. Another popular misconception about the Peak District is that it is a region of 'peaks'. Surprisingly there are few hills over 610m/2000ft, and Kinder Scout, which is the highest at 636m/2088ft, is a plateau as opposed to a peak. The name is derived from

Carl Walk and Higger Tor, Walk 5

Anglo-Saxon times when a local tribe known as the Pecsaetans called the area Peacland.

The Peak District National Park receives an estimated 22 million visits a year, which makes it the second most visited national park in the world after Mount Fuji in Japan. Its magnetic quality is assisted by the fact that half the population of England lives within 100km/60 miles of the Peak District borders, in areas including the conurbations of Manchester, Sheffield, Nottingham, Stoke and Derby. The latter is the county city of Derbyshire, and home to the car and aero-engine manufacturer Rolls Royce and to Royal Crown Derby porcelain. The south of the county receives far fewer tourists and remains less well-known despite its outstanding natural beauty and a wealth of historic houses and parklands. This book visits many of these

properties, including Hardwick Hall, Bolsover Castle, Kedleston Hall, Calke Abbey, Wingfield Manor, Melbourne Hall, Shipley Hall and Elvaston Castle. Taken as a whole, Derbyshire has not only a memorable natural splendour but also a great array of tourist attractions spread liberally across the county and providing endless interest for all the family.

HOW TO USE THIS GUIDE

This book is a collection of 60 circular, easy to moderate, day or half-day walks from across the county. They range in distance from 4km/2½ miles to 15.5km/9½ miles and are suitable for individuals and families. Each walk includes famed beauty spots and attractions and leaves plenty of scope to explore some of the less visited areas. Each is linked to a main historical theme, and the walks have been arranged in a rough chronological

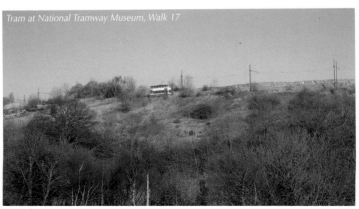
Tram at National Tramway Museum, Walk 17

Hollins Cross and Lose Hill from Edale, Walk 4

order according to the selected theme, so that you are literally walking through layers of history and treading in the footsteps of past generations. Information on the theme of the walk and other points of interest precedes the route instructions for each trail. Where appropriate, telephone numbers are provided for the tourist attractions so you can check opening times, ticket prices and so on. A map of the route is included, taken from the OS Explorer 1:50,000 series. It is strongly recommended that you read the whole of the route instructions before setting out on any walk so that you are aware of the precise nature of the route, including any steeper sections, stiles and so forth.

GEOLOGY

The changing topography of Derbyshire can be explained by its geology as the county has four main distinct regions. This varied geology is also reflected in the building materials and styles of architecture in the various towns and villages of the Peak District.

In the north of the county, in what has become known as the Dark Peak, there are sandstone moorlands. The sandstone, more commonly known as **gritstone**, forms a horseshoe shape so that, for example, along its eastern edge there is a dramatic 20km/12 mile gritstone edge running along the Derwent Valley. Today these crags are often teeming with rock climbers, but in the past this rock was used to make millstones and grindstones and has become known as **millstone grit**. Examples of discarded millstones can be found in the Hathersage area below Stanage Edge and around Bolehill Quarry. Its most frequent use, though, has been as a building stone.

Millstone grit is insoluble but porous, so it absorbs water which often seeps through the grit to the less porous shales below, producing springs. Grit and shales are less hard than the limestone of the southern

13

View from Monsal Head, Walk 38

Peak District, known as the White Peak, so the rivers here have worn much wider valleys. The acid soil and harsher, wetter weather in the upland Dark Peak provide their unique landscape of bleak and windswept peat moorland, gritstone escarpments and rugged gritstone tors.

South of the millstone grit of the Dark Peak is the **carboniferous limestone** of the White Peak, or the Derbyshire Dales as it is also known, which runs roughly from Ashbourne to Castleton. In the Dark Peak, as mentioned, shales underlie the millstone grit. Shale outcrops can also be found on the fringe of the limestone White Peak. Shale splits very easily when exposed to frost. As a friable material often interbedded with sandstone, it is vulnerable to landslip. Mam Tor is a good example of this problem, where the A625 has now

been closed for a number of years due to landslip.

Limestone has fissures and is slightly soluble in water, therefore the rivers have been able to carve deep narrow valleys, which has resulted in some of the most spectacular riverside scenery in this country, such as in Dovedale. Sometimes the rivers have found a route underground, creating caverns and leaving dry valleys behind. At Winnats Pass near Castleton it is believed that a cave system has collapsed to produce a deep narrow gorge.

The limestone of the White Peak is all around you in the drystone walls dividing the fields, the crags along the deep dales, the weird rock formations in the valleys and the many quarries which have extracted (or still are extracting) stone for commercial use. Unlike the Dark Peak the much softer

White Peak is able to support grassland used for farming, and an abundant range of flowers and plants.

Northeast Derbyshire has a belt of **magnesian limestone** running along its eastern edge by the Nottinghamshire border, which has resulted, for example, in the gorge and caves at Creswell Crags. Much of the remaining part of northeast Derbyshire has developed as a result of its vast underlying coal measures and the growth of the associated industry during the Industrial Revolution. In the Peak District any coal measures found were only near the surface and the coal was of very poor quality, so all such mining activity had ceased here by the early twentieth century.

South of Derby and Ashbourne is an area of **clay and sandstone**, providing a much more gentle countryside.

HISTORY

This outline of Derbyshire's history is designed to show how the various walks in this book fit into the overall picture of the county throughout the centuries, reflecting its changing economic activities and cultures over the years.

At the end of the Ice Age Britain was still connected to the continent, and nomadic man, who was a hunter-gatherer, would follow herds to Britain at certain times of the year. Creswell Crags on the Derbyshire/Nottinghamshire border is recognised as the most northerly known inhabited place from the **Palaeolithic period (Old Stone Age)** between 45,000 and 10,000 years ago. As the

Hardwick Hall, Walk 19

River Derwent at Baslow, Walk 3

ice melted, Britain became an island around 8000 years ago.

The years 8000 to 4000 BC are known as the **Mesolithic period (Middle Stone Age)**. After the Ice Age nomadic man came in increasing numbers to the Dark Peak. By 4500 BC man could be described as semi-nomadic, visiting the Pennine uplands in the summer and moving east in the winter. It is now believed that fires once thought to be accidental were in fact created deliberately to clear what was then forested land for grazing and crop growth. This land management may even explain the lack of trees in the Dark Peak and the development of the peat bogs at a later stage. Evidence of Mesolithic man can still be found in the Dark Peak today where it is possible to find microliths, which are tiny flakes of flint from hunting tools.

The final period of the Stone Age, the **Neolithic period (New Stone Age)** from 4000 to 2000 BC, saw the gradual transition from hunter-gatherer to farmer, and permanent settlements began to appear in the White Peak around 3000 BC. The fertile soil and abundance of springs provided an ideal combination for growing crops and grazing sheep, cattle and pigs. During the late Neolithic/early Bronze Age, man built a number of stone circles in Derbyshire and also earthwork barrows, which usually contained a stone chambered tomb below it. At this point it is worth mentioning one of the paradoxes of the Peak District, where tumuli carrying the suffix 'low', from the Old English *hlaw* meaning burial mound, actually denotes a high point. Derbyshire's most impressive Neolithic monument is Arbor Low, the 'Stonehenge of the

North'. Minninglow provides an excellent example of a chambered tomb from this period.

The **Bronze Age** from 2000 to 700 BC is known for its emergence of the Beaker people, whose culture is hallmarked by their highly decorated pottery and bronze. The Beaker people settled widely up the valleys of the Derwent, Wye and Trent. The best-preserved remains are of a settlement on Stanton Moor in the Derwent Valley where the Nine Ladies Stone Circle can be seen. Another important site is on the opposite side of the Derwent Valley on the gritstone edges around Curbar, and more recently a site has come to light at Swarkestone on the Trent. Most of the stone circles and round barrows in Derbyshire relate to the early Bronze Age. It is estimated that there are some 500 barrows in the Peak District, many of which were somewhat clumsily excavated by Victorian archaeologists

such as Thomas Bateman, although his collection has been saved and can be seen at Sheffield City Museum.

Until recently it was thought that the remains of hill forts scattered around Derbyshire's Peak District were mainly from the **Iron Age** period of 700 BC to AD 50 but it is now thought more likely that they date to the late Bronze Age. Mam Tor, Carl Wark, Fin Cop and Burr Tor provide the main examples. It was also previously believed that they were entirely defensive structures for the Iron Age Brigante tribe who inhabited most of northern England but they were probably also used for other purposes. They may well have offered a summer place to watch over the herds of livestock and provide a tribal meeting place.

The **Romans** moved north of the River Trent to secure their northern border in early AD 70, and this also allowed them to exploit and protect

Kedleston Hall, Walk 28

for themselves the rich lead deposits of the Peak District. They established two forts for military purposes at Brough (Navio) in the Hope Valley and at Melandra near Glossop at the entrance to the Longdendale Valley. A road network was also built across the Peak District linking these two forts and other forts around the region. The centre of Roman lead production is thought to have been Lutudarum, and this name has been found on Roman pig or ingots of lead. The location of Lutudarum has always remained a mystery but is thought to be in the Wirksworth/Carsington area. When Carsington Reservoir was being constructed in the 1980s some archaeologists felt that they had uncovered the elusive site but the evidence is far from conclusive.

Military settlement by the Romans in Derbyshire was followed by an element of civilian settlement but there were no grand luxurious villas such as the ones established further south. Civilian settlements grew up around the two forts, and the Romans discovered the warm thermal waters at Buxton and established a spa resort called Aquae Armenetia. The remains of their baths were discovered when The Crescent was built in the 1800s. Romano-British people, descendants of those living in Britain during the Iron Age, also built small farmsteads such as Roystone Grange at Ballidon, The Burrs at Chelmorton, Chee Tor above Miller's Dale, Littlehay Grange Farm at Ockbrook near Derby and Little Chester (Derventio) near Derby.

After the withdrawal of the Romans in the early fifth century came the **Dark Ages**, a time for which there is scant historical detail

Hathersage, Walk 49

available and particularly in respect of Derbyshire. During the fifth and sixth centuries England was made up of numerous small kingdoms which frequently fought one another over territories. By the seventh century there were effectively three kingdoms – Northumbria, Mercia and Wessex – with what is now Derbyshire falling under Mercia. In the Peak District, however, there was a separate isolated culture called Pecsaetan, meaning 'dwellers of the Peak'. The earliest written record of the existence of this culture came in the late seventh century when the 'Tribal Hidage' was drawn up to assess the taxable value of the Kingdom of Mercia.

The Anglo-Saxons then began to penetrate England and in AD 827 they defeated Mercia. Next came the Viking raids and annexation of Mercia in AD 874 and the founding of Derby. 'Danelaw' was governed from York, and Derby was the local administrative centre. In AD 920 Edward the Elder retook the region after Derby had already fallen to his sister Elfreda two years earlier. Edward built a burh (fortress) near Bakewell which was the scene in AD 920 of a major 'summit' meeting between King Edward the Elder and the kings of Danish Northumbria, Wales and Scotland at which borders were settled. The site of the burh still remains a source of speculation today. It was Edward's successors who around AD 1000 split the country into the counties we know today. Interestingly Derbyshire

was the last county to be created and this probably reflected its position as an unimportant border.

Derbyshire does, however, have some outstanding survivors from the Dark Ages in the form of decorative Christian stone preaching crosses, used before churches were built, and tombstones. The best-preserved example of a stone cross is in the churchyard at Eyam, with others in churchyards at Hope and Bakewell. There are tombstone slabs at Wirksworth and Bakewell, and at Repton an Anglo-Saxon crypt survives.

From the *Domesday Book*, which was put together in 1086, 20 years after the **Norman Conquest**, it is clear that there was already extensive occupation of Derbyshire. William the Conqueror granted substantial land in Derbyshire to one of his most trusted knights, William Peverel, who may have been his illegitimate son. Peverel administered the Royal Forest of the Peak as a hunting reserve for kings and princes from Peveril Castle. The prominent and impressive ruins of this castle stand above the village of Castleton, which was developed as a planned medieval town but never grew to be of any size or importance. Peverel also looked after another of the royal forests in the Derwent Valley from his castle at Duffield. He also had castles in Derbyshire at Bolsover, Codnor and Mackworth. Evidence of Norman motte and bailey castles exist at Pilsbury near Hartington and close to Bakewell, and the Normans

Robin Hood's Stride, Walk 32

also built a castle at Melbourne. Peveril Castle has undoubtedly best survived the ravages of time and man; others such as Codnor survive in fragments, whilst Melbourne and Duffield have completely disappeared.

The thirteenth century saw the building of many great abbeys and monasteries throughout England, but Derbyshire is not well endowed with abbatial remains, and the chancel arch of Dale Abbey represents the main relic of this period. Most of the Norman church architecture has disappeared in subsequence and in particular as a result of Victorian rebuilding programmes, which makes the church at Melbourne a very special example of relatively original Norman architecture. Not only is this one of the most important churches in England but it is also one of the most visually impressive.

During the **Middle Ages** Derbyshire's economy and wealth centred on lead and wool. Certain villages expanded under the profits of sheep farming and lead mining and built fine churches. From a time when we have no hard statistics on economic growth, the level of new building work is a reasonable guide to the prosperity or otherwise of the time. The twelfth to the fourteenth centuries appear to have been a time of expansion. Some towns and villages grew with the granting of market rights, such as Bakewell, Tideswell, Ashbourne, Hartington and Monyash, and were often more important places than they are today, with their prosperity being reflected in the size and magnificence of their churches. Tideswell is the classic example as its very large and grand church, the 'Cathedral of the Peak', seems out of proportion to the village itself but was built from the profits of wool and lead. The Middle Ages was also a time when monastic houses from outside Derbyshire established sheep granges, particularly in the

White Peak. Today virtually all farms with the name grange in them were originally church property. The church even worked lead mines such as the one that Repton Abbey owned at Wirksworth.

A series of poor harvests and the Black Death in the mid-fourteenth century seem to have been the catalyst for difficult times, and over the next two centuries no significant church building took place. Certain landowning families were, however, beginning to demonstrate their wealth and power by building grand mansions. For example, the Vernon family (later Dukes of Rutland) were responsible for Haddon Hall, and Lord Cromwell, Chancellor to Henry VI, built Wingfield Manor as a hunting retreat. As Henry VI was an infant at the time Cromwell was Chancellor, he was effectively one of the rulers and most powerful men in England. As landowners began to take in more and more land the first enclosure of medieval open fields took place. Medieval patterns of enclosure can be seen today in the White Peak around villages such as Chelmorton and Monyash.

Little of the extensive land and property of the church survived the **Dissolution of the Monasteries** in 1538, and large estates passed into the hands of some of the great Derbyshire families, who displayed their wealth and power by building palatial mansions. The Cavendishes, who were later created the Dukes of Devonshire after the fourth earl's role in overthrowing the Catholic James II

Peveril Castle from Cave Dale, Walk 8

River Derwent, Grindleford and Froggatt Edge, Walk 3

and offering the Crown to William of Orange and Mary in the Glorious Revolution of 1688, were connected with Chatsworth House, Bolsover Castle and Hardwick Hall. The Vernons, later Dukes of Rutland, were associated with Haddon Hall and Sudbury Hall. John Coke and his descendants lived at Melbourne Hall, including the Second Lord Melbourne, who was Queen Victoria's first prime minister, and Lord Palmerston who was her second. Some of the other great Derbyshire families mentioned in this guide are the Curzons from Kedleston Hall, the Harpur Crewes from Calke Abbey, the Stanhopes at Elvaston Castle, the Fitzherberts at Tissington Hall, the Miller Mundys at Shipley Hall and the Drury-Lowes at Locko Hall. Often in the grounds of these estates delightful

estate villages were built such as Edensor at Chatsworth or Osmaston near Ashbourne.

It was a member of the Cavendish family, Sir William Cavendish, who was appointed to oversee the dissolution of the monasteries in Derbyshire. Through this appointment he was granted church land and was in a position to buy other land cheaply. Sir William was to be the second of the four husbands of Bess of Hardwick, who was one of the most controversial figures in the **reign of Queen Elizabeth I**. Indeed she outlived all her husbands to became the richest and most powerful person in Elizabethan England after the Queen. William and Bess built the house that stood at Chatsworth before the current house was erected, but Bess is primarily associated with the hall she built at

Hardwick, 'more glass than wall', after the death of her fourth husband, George Talbot, Sixth Earl of Shrewsbury.

George had been head of one of the oldest and richest families in England, and was saddled by Elizabeth I with the task of acting as gaoler to Mary Queen of Scots from 1569 to 1584. Mary was moved around some of George's properties including Sheffield Castle, Chatsworth House and Wingfield Manor. It was while she was held at Wingfield Manor that she allegedly met Anthony Babington, whose family lived at Dethick. It is said he made visits to her dressed as a gypsy and that he conceived what has gone down in history as the Babington Plot to murder Elizabeth I so that Mary, her

heir, could take the throne and promote Catholicism. Following the discovery of his plans he was executed, and soon after Mary received the same fate. Catholic persecution was rife throughout the reign of Elizabeth I. It was during the year of the Spanish Armada in 1588 when religious tensions were further heightened that Sir Thomas Fitzherbert of Padley Hall was found harbouring two Catholic priests. The priests were hung, drawn and quartered after their arrest, and the gatehouse of Padley Hall, which was later converted to a chapel, now holds an annual pilgrimage at the chapel to commemorate the two Padley martyrs.

During the **Civil War**, which commenced in 1642, Derbyshire as a whole saw little fighting, although

Haddon Hall, Walk 16

Wingfield Manor was besieged and Bolsover Castle ruined. When the plague returned in 1665 to devastate the country's population, the village of Eyam received a visitation. Eyam is famed as the Plague Village because of the brave decision taken by its inhabitants to impose a voluntary quarantine upon themselves to contain the spread of the disease. The Fourth Earl of Devonshire's part in the Glorious Revolution of 1688 to replace the Catholic James II with the Protestant William of Orange and Mary led to him being created First Duke of Devonshire, as mentioned. The hopes of the supporters of James and his heirs, the Jacobites, finally came to an end when his grandson Bonnie Prince Charlie ended his march on London in 1745 at Swarkestone Bridge in Derbyshire.

Nelson's victory at the Battle of Trafalgar in 1805 against Napoleon Bonaparte and then Wellington's ending of the **Napoleonic Wars** at the Battle of Waterloo in 1815 marked the start of a severe economic depression and discontent was rife. The village of Pentrich is closely linked with the scenes of England's last revolution in 1817. The revolt was soon quashed and severe punishments were handed out. Its ringleaders were the last men in England to receive a sentence to be hung, drawn and quartered. Holloway, another Derbyshire village, was for many years one of the homes of Florence Nightingale, the famous Lady of the Lamp who tended the soldiers of the Crimean War in the mid-nineteenth century and provided the catalyst for nursing to become a profession.

THE SHAPING OF PRESENT-DAY DERBYSHIRE

The present-day character of the Peak District began to take shape during the seventeenth and eighteenth centuries as many of the farms we see today were built or rebuilt of either gritstone or limestone depending on their location. This, alongside the building of many halls, illustrates a return to affluence and confidence that had not been seen since the plague hit England in the mid-fourteenth century. During the eighteenth and early nineteenth centuries fields were enclosed as part of the Enclosure Movement. In the White Peak this took the form of miles of drystone walls, a manmade feature, which now blend so naturally into the scenery.

Mineral extraction, particularly of **lead**, had been important to the White Peak for centuries but only on a minor scale and usually in conjunction with farming. The first half of the eighteenth century was the most prosperous time for lead mining and this is reflected in the growth of certain villages and their churches. Mineral wealth was also important to the gentry. For example, it was from the profits of his Ecton copper mines, just outside Derbyshire, that the Fifth Duke of Devonshire began

Magpie Lead Mine near Sheldon, Walk 29

the transformation of Buxton into a spa resort. There has also been much quarrying of other raw materials throughout the county. In the Dark Peak, for example, gritstone has been used in building materials and millstones. Limestone quarrying is another of Derbyshire's old industries, which continues today and is very much the subject of controversial debate, because whilst it may scar the landscape it also provides employment.

As the demand for lead increased the mines started to be dug deeper underground. Eventually this meant that the water table was reached and a constant battle was then fought and often lost to keep the volume of water in the mine to a minimum. Pumping alone usually proved to be inadequate, and this meant abandoning the mine or dewatering by driving a sough, an underground drainage channel, sometimes several miles to a

river valley. The Cromford sough, which ran from a Wirksworth lead mine to the River Derwent, was later used by Richard Arkwright to power his mill at Cromford. It was built in 1688 at a massive cost for the time of £30,000. Lead mining as an industry was, however, effectively finished by the end of the nineteenth century. The White Peak is littered with the remains of centuries of work, the best preserved being the Magpie Lead Mine near Sheldon.

Derbyshire and especially the Peak District was slow to lose its remoteness. By the early eighteenth century the Peak District was crossed by a series of **packhorse routes** which had barely changed since medieval times, carrying salt and cheese from Cheshire and returning with lead and lime. Today some of the original packhorse bridges still remain such as at Three Shires Head, marking the converging boundaries of Derbyshire,

25

Cromford Canal, Walk 34

Staffordshire and Cheshire. Derbyshire did not possess any navigable rivers, and as industrialisation began to gain pace the inadequacies of the transport system were highlighted, so between 1730 and 1830 a network of **turnpike roads** was established. On the whole, however, whilst this improved passenger transport it was still not suitable for the movement of bulk cargoes.

This situation improved greatly after the father of canal mania, James Brindley, supervised work on Britain's first modern canal for the Duke of Bridgewater from his Lancashire coal mines into Manchester during 1761. Brindley was born at Tunstead near Buxton. Josiah Wedgwood, the Staffordshire potter, then asked Brindley to construct a **canal** linking the important worldwide trading ports of Liverpool and Hull via the Mersey and Humber. This 150km/93mile route, originally called the Grand

Trunk Canal, was built between 1766 and 1777 and is now known as the Trent and Mersey Canal. A number of connections were then made into this main trade artery from Derbyshire and an important inland port grew up at Shardlow, several kilometres from where the Trent meets the Trent and Mersey Canal.

Other canals built in Derbyshire were the Chesterfield Canal, again built under the initial supervision of Brindley before his death, and Benjamin Outram had a hand in building the Derby Canal, the Cromford Canal and the Peak Forest Canal. Outram was also one of the founders of the famous Butterley Ironworks close to the Cromford Canal. Later William Jessop, who had been chief engineer for the Cromford Canal, with Outram as his assistant, became involved with the Butterley Ironworks, and his son William Jessop junior took the company on to even

26

greater things. Another of William Jessop senior's sons, Josiah, was responsible for the first **railway** in the Peak District, the Cromford and High Peak line, built in 1830 and joining the Cromford Canal to the Peak Forest Canal. Originally it was intended to be a canal but technically it was realised that this was not possible. Horses were initially used to pull wagons up the step inclines but these were later replaced by steam-powered beam engines.

Other railways through the region quickly followed and by 1840 there were three railway companies operating lines to Derby from Nottingham, Leeds and Birmingham, and five years later these had amalgamated to become the Midland Railway Company based at Derby. In 1863 came the eventual completion of the profitable Midland Line from Manchester to London. This now forms a section of the Monsal Trail along the Wye Valley. Another important railway line across the county was the Great Central Line built in 1847 from Sheffield to Glossop, passing through the Woodhead Tunnels and along the Longdendale Valley, which now serves as the Longdendale Trail. Also the Hope Valley Line constructed in 1894, linking Sheffield to Stockport via Edale, remains today, as it always has been, a popular ramblers' route.

Ironically the waters of Derbyshire, which contributed greatly to the downfall of the lead industry, provided the power for mills and enabled the next phase of industrial development, particularly along the Derwent Valley, which attracted the first industrialists to the county. In 1718 John Lombe built his silk mill at

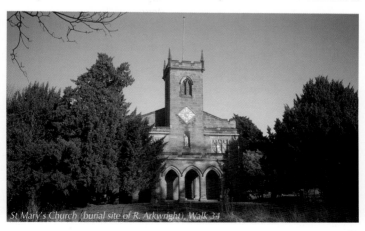

St Mary's Church (burial site of R. Arkwright). Walk 34

Derby, but later **Richard Arkwright** came to isolated Cromford on the River Derwent in 1771 and built the world's first **water-powered spinning mill**. This was also the first mass-production factory in the world and it uniquely incorporated a model village for its workforce. Jedediah Strutt, Arkwright's partner at Cromford, then dissolved their partnership in 1781 and set up his own successful empire downstream at Belper. Here his son William built one of the world's first fire-resistant buildings, which still stands today and is of enormous importance in industrial archaeology terms. Due to its geographical position Cromford may not have gone on to rival Manchester and

Willersley Castle, Walk 34

Leeds, but the Derwent Valley was undoubtedly a cradle of the Industrial Revolution and is now designated the National Heritage Corridor seeking World Heritage Site status. By the end of the eighteenth century there were 30 cotton mills in Derbyshire, and Arkwright went on to build other mills at Cressbrook and near Bakewell. Other textile centres sprang up at Glossop under the patronage of the Duke of Norfolk and at New Mills initially, around the confluence of the rivers Sett and Goyt, then a second phase of building took place along the Peak Forest Canal when steam power came to the forefront.

When the transition was later made from water power to steam, factories moved from the rivers to the source of the raw materials which generated the steam. This took Derbyshire's industrialisation away from its centre to the northeastern corner where there were abundant coal supplies and also ironstone and limestone. This area along with South Yorkshire grew during the late nineteenth and early twentieth centuries to become an enormous **supplier of coal and producer of iron and steel** until the collapse of this as an industrial base in the 1980s.

Tourism today is a major industry for Derbyshire, which has grown from the sixteenth century and has gathered great pace in the last two centuries. On the first map of the Peak District, drawn by Saxton in 1577, several of the area's natural curiosities

Buxton, Walk 56

were marked on the map. Later in 1678 the political philosopher Thomas Hobbes, at this time a tutor at Chatsworth House, published what was in effect the first guidebook of the Peak District, describing the 'Wonders' of the Peak. His wonders included Chatsworth, Mam Tor, Eldon Hole, Buxton Wells, Poole's Hole and Devil's Arse (Castleton). The co-author of this book was Charles Cotton of Beresford Hall near Hartington, who also co-authored *The Compleat Angler* with Izaac Walton.

It was the start of the growth of Buxton by the Fifth Duke of Devonshire from Chatsworth and his successors, along with Matlock Bath, as spa resorts during Georgian times that really began Derbyshire's tourist trade. The upper and middle classes came to 'take the waters' at these resorts and view the wonders of nature. Although neither was to

become another Bath or Cheltenham, enormous investments were made to build a full-blown Victorian tourist infrastructure around each. The coming of the railways was another significant factor in the growth of the Victorian passion for tourism, as by the 1880s the likes of Buxton and Matlock Bath were accessible by the popular masses. Other areas also began to draw the Victorian crowds, such as Castleton and Dovedale.

Regions of ever increasing population, with the growth of the industrial areas of Sheffield, Manchester, Nottingham and Derby, began to surround Derbyshire, and the workers from these smoky cities and towns found the Peak District a welcome breath of fresh air and escape route for weekend day trips. This recreational lung provided by the Peak District to so many people was one of the reasons why the region became one of the main battlegrounds for the 'access to the countryside' campaign during the 1920s and 30s. At that time the Dark Peak's high moorland was the strictly private game reserve of a few wealthy landowners. Events culminated in 1932 with the famous Mass Trespass of 400 ramblers onto the forbidden moorland of Kinder Scout, starting out from Hayfield. This event and related campaign work, along with the ever increasing pressures of visitor numbers, undoubtedly provided a catalyst for the Peak District to become Britain's first designated national park in 1951. Since then access agreements have opened up areas of high sombre moorland in the Dark Peak for the more intrepid bogtrotters, including the Pennine Way which starts at Edale and was Britain's first long-distance footpath in 1965. Likewise the much more gentle dales of the White Peak have seen the creation of the High Peak Trail, the Tissington Trail and the Monsal Trail which are now well-established leisure trails for all abilities, using disused railway lines. Just to prove that 'roam' was not built in a day, the 'access to roam' campaign was again at the top of the political agenda as the last millennium drew to a close and the government confirmed it was pressing ahead with its 'right to roam' proposals.

The twentieth century has also seen manmade changes to the landscape in the form of the construction of **reservoirs** to quench the thirst of the inhabitants of the sprawling cities and towns. Along with the building of many of these reservoirs came the planting of blocks of conifer plantations, especially in the Dark Peak, for example in the Upper Derwent Valley, the Goyt Valley and the

Litton View from Monsal Head, Walk 13 or 38

Longdendale Valley. Later other large reservoirs were built at Carsington in the White Peak and Staunton Harold Reservoir at the southern tip of Derbyshire. All of these provide not only a vital water supply but in recent decades have also served as recreational facilities for the general public.

For centuries Derbyshire sat isolated in Middle England as a border of varying kinds but never as a frontier. It was the pioneering work of men such as Richard Arkwright at Cromford and the Duke of Devonshire at Buxton in developing a spa resort which began to bring the county into the mainstream of English life. Today the county has much to offer the tourist and must learn new ways to deal with the ever increasing numbers of visitors descending upon it, to preserve it for future generations. As we move forward in the twenty-first century there is a delicate balancing act to perform, and transport, quarrying and farming are three hot issues to resolve in the new millennium.

CUSTOMS

Derbyshire people still practise a number of customs, the most famous and popular being **well dressing**, which takes place throughout Derbyshire during spring and summer. It is a little unclear as to when this custom began but it is now generally accepted that it was a pagan Celtic ceremony giving thanks for water. The practice was revived in the early seventeenth century at Tissington when water remained in the wells even after a prolonged drought. Traditionally Tissington has the first well dressing of the year on Ascension Day with many Derbyshire villages then following.

Flower petals and other natural materials are painstakingly pressed into a wooden frame containing wet clay, usually depicting a religious scene but local or topical scenes are also made. The dressings are placed around the village and draw large crowds before they are destroyed by the elements of the weather and are taken down again.

Another floral tribute is the **Castleton Garland Day** which takes place on Oak Apple Day on 29 May. This pagan tradition was probably originally some sort of fertility rite celebrating the end of winter. During the seventeenth century the ceremony adopted a different purpose to commemorate the restoration of the Monarchy. May 29th became known as Oak Apple Day in remembrance of Charles II hiding in an oak tree to escape the Roundheads. The ceremony involves a 'king' on horseback covered in a garland of flowers so that only his legs are visible and his 'consort' being paraded around the village before hoisting the garland to the top of the tower of St Edmund's Church.

On Shrove Tuesday and Ash Wednesday **Ashbourne** plays **Shrovetide Football**. It is the last place in the country where mass football is still

31

Stepping Stones, Dovedale, Walk 58

played through the streets at Shrovetide. This ancient game is played between the Up'ards and the Down'ards of Ashbourne with team membership historically depending on which side of the River Henmore you were born. The players are collectively known as the hug, with the old name for this game being hugball. The game is preceded by a lunch and the ball is 'turned up' at 2pm. The goals are 3 miles/2km apart, and if a goal is scored before 5pm another ball is turned up. Once a ball is goaled after 5pm the game ends, although play can continue up to 10pm. Play is mainly in the streets and fields surrounding the river using attractively painted balls filled with cork shavings and weighing just under 4lb/1.8kg.

A commemoration service is held just outside the village of **Eyam** every August to remember the brave action of the villagers in imposing a quarantine upon themselves when they received a visitation from the **Plague** in 1665. Another commemoration service takes place at Padley Chapel to celebrate the **Padley Martyrs** who were discovered hiding at Padley Hall and were hung, drawn and quartered for their Catholic beliefs during the sixteenth century.

WALK 1
Creswell Crags

Distance:	9km/5½ miles
Start:	Creswell Crags Visitor Centre off the B6042 which runs between the A616 at Creswell and the A60
Map:	OS Explorer 28 Sherwood Forest
Terrain:	Easy walking along fields, country lanes and tracks

Following the discovery of human remains by archaeologists in the late nineteenth century this 'miniature Cheddar Gorge' has become one of Europe's most important sites for palaeontology and archaeology, ranking alongside Stonehenge and Hadrian's Wall, although from the public perspective it is not as well known. Creswell Crags Visitor Centre provides an interpretation and appreciation of the importance of the ravine in the evolution of man through interactive exhibits.

Creswell Crags is a dramatic magnesian limestone gorge honeycombed with caves, which bisects the Nottinghamshire/ northeast Derbyshire border. The animal and plant remains found in the caves provide a unique time-capsule and tell the fascinating story of the origins of human life during the last Ice Age.

Creswell Crags

The entire gorge is a Scheduled Ancient Monument and a Site of Special Scientific Interest. From the first Victorian archaeologists, however, the crags have suffered from poor and inappropriate management, such as the use of dynamite to blast the caves and a road and sewage works built in the gorge. There are now plans for substantial development in the gorge and surrounding area under a project called the Creswell Initiative (details in the visitor centre). The Heritage Lottery Fund is to provide the resources to implement the higher standards of management, conservation, infrastructure and interpretation that the site deserves to repair the damage done in the last century.

ROUTE INSTRUCTIONS

1 From the visitor centre car park, which is on the route of the Robin Hood Way, walk past the visitor centre and take the path immediately off to the left signposted 'To The Crags'. Walk past the sewage works on your left up to Crags Pond. There is a path down each side of the pond and either option may be taken.

At the end of the pond turn left and soon climb a stile and continue uphill for 20m to a waymark post. Here turn sharp left and on reaching the brow of the hill look for a stile in the far left-hand corner of the field.

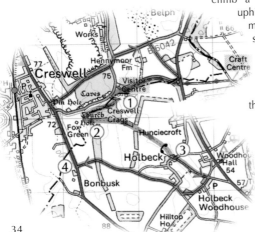

2 Climb the stile and follow the wall edge on your left which later becomes a wire fence. The clear path then begins to swing right to a stile. Climb the stile and follow the waymarked path straight ahead across several fields until you reach the road in Holbeck.

3 Turn left and then immediately right at a sign-post onto a surfaced tree-lined track. Halfway down this track on the right-hand side is St Winifred's Church, which is the private church of the Portland family from nearby Welbeck Abbey. On meeting a road leave the Robin Hood Way by turning right. Walk through Holbeck Woodhouse and where the road forks bear to the right. At a T-junction turn right and walk to another T-junction. Cross over the road and follow the signposted track in front of you which is hedged on both sides. This clear track takes you to the A616.

4 At the road turn right and follow the footpath along the right-hand side of the A616 into Creswell. Shortly after crossing a road junction off to the right which leads to the Crags, turn right at a signpost and head up towards Bank House Farm.

Follow the track around the right-hand perimeter of the farm, which shortly becomes hedged on both sides. Turn left on reaching the B6042 and follow it around a right-hand bend. Continue past the driveway to Hennymoor Farm and 100m further on turn right onto a green lane and walk to the A60. Turn right onto this road and then right again in 30m onto a track by a lodge, which returns you to the visitor centre.

Refreshments:	Creswell Crags Visitor Centre
Toilets:	Creswell Crags Visitor Centre
Key Features:	Creswell Crags and its visitor centre (01909 720378)

WALK 2
Arbor Low Stone Circle

Arbor Low, often referred to as the 'Stonehenge of the North', is a sizeable and important henge in the care of English Heritage and located on a large plateau south of Monyash. A henge is a circular earthwork of banks and ditches dating to the late Neolithic and early Bronze Age, approximately 2000 BC.

Distance:	10.5km/6½ miles
Start:	Hartington Old Signal Box on the Tissington Trail off the B5054 near Hartington
Map:	OS Explorer OL24 The Peak District White Peak Area
Terrain:	Very easy walking on trails and country lanes

Arbor Low henge is roughly 48m/157ft in diameter and 2m/6½ft high. In the centre is a stone circle containing around 50 large limestone slabs. As the stones are lying down, in archaeological terms this is known as a recumbent stone circle, and although there is disagreement as to whether the stones ever stood up the current thinking is that they did. At the centre of the stone circle there are several even larger stones which formed the core where ceremonies could be conducted hidden from view.

The exact time that Arbor Low was built and its purpose are the subject of much debate, but the henge is generally described as being Neolithic with a later, Bronze Age barrow or burial mound superimposed on the southern side of the embankment.

Several fields away from Arbor Low is an even earlier Neolithic monument, Gib Hill, which is a long barrow dating to around 3000 BC with a Bronze Age barrow again superimposed onto it.

ROUTE INSTRUCTIONS

1 Walk back to the entrance to the car park and down a lane to reach the B5054. Turn right onto the road and in 200m bear left onto a walled track which leads to the A515. The route continues

straight ahead on the track at the other side of this busy main road, but the Jug and Glass Inn is 100m to the right. The track reaches the High Peak Trail at a crossroads in 300m.

2 Turn left through a gate onto the High Peak Trail and follow it past the junction with the Tissington Trail to reach the Parsley Hay car park 300m further on. Here leave the trail and walk to the entrance to the car park. Turn left and left again onto the A515. Cross this busy road with care and turn right in 20m at a T-junction. Then in 150m turn right at a T-junction and follow the lane to the entrance to Upper Oldhams Farm in 1.5km/1 mile where there is an English Heritage sign for Arbor Low. Access is on a permissive path and a small charge may be made. Turn right up the farm driveway and through the farmyard to two gates. Climb a stile to the left of the gates and then turn left to follow a field edge with a wall on the left. Climb another stile to reach Arbor Low.

3 Retrace your steps to the Parsley Hay car park and turn left back onto the High Peak Trail. At the junction with the Tissington Trail in 300m bear to the right onto this trail and follow it back to Hartington Signal Box where you step off the trail to the left back into the car park.

Refreshments:	Hartington Old Signal Box, Jug and Glass Inn on the A515 and Parsley Hay car park
Toilets:	Hartington Old Signal Box car park and Parsley Hay car park
Key Features:	Sections of the Tissington and High Peak Trails; Hartington Old Signal Box Information Centre; Arbor Low Stone Circle

WALK 3
Baslow, Curbar and Froggatt Edges

The Baslow, Curbar and Froggatt edges form a magnificent long gritstone escarpment which stretches along the eastern rim of the Derwent Valley and is a prominent landmark in the area. It was also the home of Bronze Age man. This natural wall to the valley provides fine and popular rock climbing country and extensive views.

Distance:	15.5km/9½ miles
Start:	Car park just off the A619 at Baslow
Map:	OS Explorer OL24 The Peak District White Peak Area
Terrain:	There is a gradual climb out of Baslow onto the edges followed by easy walking. This is quite a long walk, best kept for a clear day to admire the views.

Baslow grew around a fording point of the River Derwent and stands at the northern border of the Chatsworth Estate. It is unusual for a Peak District village in that it contains several thatched cottages. The village is made up of three settlements: Bridge End, Nether End and Over End. Bridge End forms the basis of the village, Nether End was developed around 1840 when it became the private northern entrance to Chatsworth and Over End evolved later due to the residential building of houses.

Baslow and Calver Edges

Eagle Stone, Baslow Edge

Recently Calver Mill has been substantially renovated to provide luxury apartments but not long ago this
large disused gritstone mill provided a very austere and
forbidding sight. Indeed its satanic profile made it a suitable substitute for Colditz Castle in the 1970s television
series. On the current mill site two Midland hosiers
leased a corn mill in 1778 and built a three-storey cotton
mill. The mill was struck by a series of disasters when a
flood washed away Calver Bridge and part of the mill
and then soon afterwards the entire structure was burnt
to the ground. Undaunted, the partners built a six-storey
mill which began production in 1804. Cotton spinning
ceased at the site in 1923 and the mill then lay dormant
until in the Second World War plant was installed for
crushing and washing fluorspar for the Sheffield steel
industry. Later the mill was used for making stainless
steel sinks before falling empty again.

ROUTE INSTRUCTIONS

1 From the car park cross over the A619 with
care and walk along Eaton Hill on the opposite

side. At the T-junction with Bar Road turn right and follow this No Through Road to the end of the houses. Continue ahead on a rough track which bends first to the right and then to the left and eventually reaches the edge of the Eastern Moors Estate. Keep ascending towards the top of the ridge and disregard any other paths until you have almost reached the Wellington Monument. Dr Wrench erected this monument in memory of the Duke of Wellington in 1866. On the opposite side of the valley is Nelson's monument on Birchin Edge.

2 At the junction of paths just before the Wellington Monument turn left onto Baslow Edge and soon pass a large solitary gritstone tor on the right known as Eagle Stone. According to legend at one time the young men of Baslow had to climb to the top of this rock to prove their manhood to the local girls before they were allowed to marry. Follow the clear path along the edge to a lane and cross over onto Curbar Edge. Maintain

Former Calver Mill

40

direction on the main path as Curbar Edge
eventually gives way to Froggatt Edge
after you have passed a yellow waymarker, which would take you down
off the edge. Instead continue onto
Froggatt Edge, passing a small
stone circle on the right to
reach the B6054.

3 Turn right onto the
road and then turn
left through a gate in
30m. Cross over a
stream and turn left at
a public footpath sign
on the edge of a car
park. Head down into
woodland and at a
fork bear left. At a
crossroad of paths
keep ahead, still
dropping downhill.
At a T-junction in front
of a wall turn left to walk
alongside the wall to a T-junction of tracks at the edge of the
woodland. Turn right and follow the
track to the B6521.

4 Turn left onto the road and in 30m, just
before Grindleford Bridge which
straddles the River Derwent, pass through
a gate on the left. Follow a grassy path
across the middle of a field to a gate.
After the gate turn right and negotiate
another gate in 50m. At a fork just after
entering trees keep to the right to walk
close to the edge of the woodland. At
the end of the woods pass through a
squeeze stile into a field. Walk across the

*River Derwent
at Baslow*

middle of the field and then follow the right-hand edge of another field. In the next field bear half right to a wall corner and then follow the wall on your left to a squeeze stile next to a gate. Spooner Lane, which is a walled track, leads to the village of Froggatt. On meeting a road in front of Hollow Froggatt Wesleyan Reform Chapel turn right onto Hollowgate to reach Froggatt Bridge over the Derwent.

5 Cross over the bridge and turn left onto the path at the opposite side and follow the riverbank to New Bridge. Cross over the road and continue along the riverside passing a weir and walking by the goit (manmade watercourse) for Calver Mill. When Calver Mill comes into view bear to the right at a fork away from the river to Stocking Farm.

6 Pass through a gate next to the farm and walk along a surfaced lane to Calver. Turn left at the road to pass the front of Calver Mill. At the far side

of Calver Bridge turn left opposite the Bridge pub onto Curbar Lane next to the church and walk steeply uphill to Curbar. At a crossroads turn right onto Cliff Lane. As the lane bends to the right climb a stile on the left just before Fir Trees Lodge, which is signposted for Baslow via Gorse Bank Farm.

7 Follow an enclosed path to a stile in front of Lane Farm. Climb the stile and turn right onto a walled track to a stile. After the stile walk alongside a wall on the right and pass through a gate. Walk to the top of a short hill and turn half right across a small field to another gate. Continue ahead across the middle of a field and keep to the right-hand edge of the next field to a squeeze stile. Walk diagonally across the field to the corner and join an enclosed track. The clear track passes through Gorse Bank Farm and then becomes a surfaced driveway back to Baslow. Turn right at a T-junction with Bar Road then left onto Ecton Hill to retrace your steps to the starting point.

Refreshments:	Pubs and cafes in Baslow and the Bridge pub at Calver
Toilets:	Car park at Baslow
Key Features:	Baslow, Curbar and Froggatt Edges; the village of Baslow; a former cotton mill at Calver

WALK 4
Edale and Mam Tor

Edale sits in the broad valley of the River Noe on the southern edge of Kinder Scout, which at 636m/2088ft is the highest point in the Peak District National Park and is home to the wildest moorland of the Dark Peak. On the other side of the valley runs a predominant ridge from Lose Hill across to Hollins Cross and then over to Mam Tor and Rushup Edge.

Distance:	10.5km/6½ miles
Start:	Car park at Edale approached from either the A625 at Hope or near the top of Winnats Pass
Map:	OS Explorer OL1 The Peak District Dark Peak Area
Terrain:	A long gradual climb from Edale onto the ridge and up to Mam Tor followed by easy walking. Wait for clear skies to complete this walk as the views are extensive.

Edale is in fact the name of the valley – the proper name of the village is Grindsbrook Booth. Strung along the valley are five ancient farming settlements or 'booths': Nether Booth, Ollerbrook Booth, Grindsbrook Booth, Barber Booth and Upper Booth. A booth was a temporary hut-like shelter for herdsmen and their cattle. Grindsbrook Booth has grown into the largest of these five settlements, complete with parish church, and has adopted the name of Edale.

Today dairy farming and stock rearing is still important to the area, but since the opening of the Sheffield to Manchester railway line in 1894 tourism has become the economic mainstay of the village. Edale is now regarded as one of the major walking centres in the country and this status has risen dramatically since the opening in 1965 of the first and most famous long-distance footpath in Britain, the Pennine Way. Edale is the start of the 434km/270 mile route to Kirk Yetholm just over the Scottish border.

Mam Tor, standing at 517m/1695ft, means 'mother mountain' but it is known locally as the Shivering Mountain as its layers of gritstone and shale have gradually crumbled to cause landslides and the resultant closure

of the A625 around it. Ringing the top of Mam Tor is the site of a late Bronze Age/early Iron Age fort. The mountain is now a very popular launch pad for hang gliders.

*Nag's Head, Edale –
the start of the
Pennine Way*

ROUTE INSTRUCTIONS

1 Turn right out of the car park and cross over a T-junction. In 50m turn left onto a public bridle-way signposted for Castleton. Follow the surfaced lane past Hardenclough Farm and then as it bends to the left at a path junction and back to the right. When the lane ends just before Greenlands climb a stile on the left next to a signpost for Hollins Cross. Follow a clear path as it climbs gradually uphill towards the top of a ridge passing through several gates. Keep ahead at a junction of paths to reach the top of the ridge 100m further on and then turn right at the crossroad of tracks to walk along the ridge towards Mam Tor. This route has now been paved in an attempt to control the erosion created from sheer overuse by walkers. The village of Castleton and the closed A625 can be seen over to

45

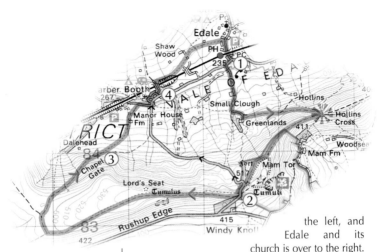

the left, and Edale and its church is over to the right. The track climbs steadily up to the trig point on Mam Tor and then drops back downhill to a road.

2 Turn left onto the road and then bear to the right onto a track in 30m to reach Rushup Edge. The track steadily climbs up to the top of the ridge. Turn left to walk along the ridge for several kilometres and when the A625 comes into view turn right at a large T-junction of paths, which is signposted for Edale. At a fork in 200m keep ahead on the main track which now starts to drop downhill heading towards Barber Booth in the valley bottom. When you reach the bottom of the hill pass through a gap at the side of a gate on the left to leave the track.

3 Head over to a stile in 20m and then continue along a grassy path dropping gently down to another stile. Follow the left-hand edge of a field to a stile. Climb the stile to walk with a wire fence on the right to a stile. Head across a field to another stile and cross over a track and maintain direction

to reach yet another stile. Follow a path between fields and then along the left-hand edge of the next field by a stream to reach a road. Turn right onto the road and then left at the T-junction onto Edale Road. Ignore a track in 10m but bear left onto the lane immediately after it through Barber Booth.

4 Twenty metres before reaching Edale Road again bear left onto a track by a signpost for Edale Station. The track bends to the left and then crosses over a railway line. Immediately after the railway line pass through a gate on the right onto a track. Just before the track bends to the left pass through a gate to the right of the track to follow the right-hand edge of a field. After the next gate head across the middle of a field to another gate and maintain direction to reach a track which leads up to Shaw Wood Farm. Cross over the track and climb some steps to negotiate a gate in 20m. Turn right at the public footpath signpost to Edale car park and pass through a gate at the side of a track to follow the left-hand edge of two fields back to

Edale and Kinder Scout from Mam Tor

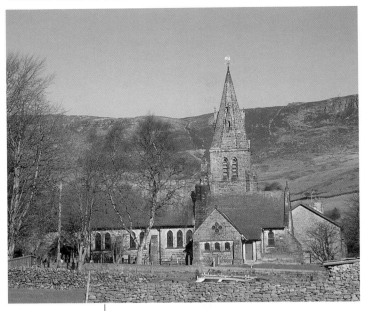

Edale with Kinder Scout behind

Edale. Turn right onto a road and pass the Ramblers Inn on the right. The car park is on the left after passing under a railway.

Refreshments: Pub and railway station at Edale

Toilets: Car park at Edale

Key Features: The valley of Edale and Mam Tor

WALK 5
Longshaw Estate and Carl Wark

Distance:	9km/5½ miles
Start:	Longshaw Estate car park off the B6055
Map:	OS Explorer OL1 The Peak District Dark Peak Area
Terrain:	Easy walking with a short sharp climb to the top of Higger Tor. There is a boggy area for a short while after Carl Wark, which can be a problem following heavy rain or snowfall.

The National Trust has maintained the 1600 acre Longshaw Estate since the early 1970s. It was once part of a much larger estate owned by the Dukes of Rutland, which was sold and broken up in 1927. Longshaw Lodge, built in 1827 as a shooting lodge, is the focal point for the estate with the National Trust Visitor Centre next to it. Today it has been converted into private flats. The area around the visitor centre is ablaze with rhododendrons in May/June. Every September on the meadow below the lodge the country's oldest sheepdog trials are held, which first took place in 1898.

ROUTE INSTRUCTIONS

1 Follow the main path from the car park and turn right at a T-junction to reach the National Trust Visitor Centre on the left. Turn right at a T-junction to reach the B6521 and cross over to a gate at the opposite side. Head downhill to a junction of paths and bear right to the A625. Cross over to join the left-hand of two routes. The path follows

A fort once stood on the prominent gritstone platform of Carl Wark, which provides an extensive view of the Derwent Valley, but the origins of the fort have remained undecided. Originally it was felt that the hill was fortified in the Iron Age but many archaeologists dispute this and believe it was built later around AD 500. Alternatively, perhaps the first defence was Iron Age and further fortifications were added in the post-Roman era.

49

a valley by Burbage Rocks to reach a road by the Upper Burbage Bridge.

2 Turn left onto the road and after the bridge climb a stile on the left in 30m. At the junction immediately in front of you bear to the right onto Fiddler's Elbow. The path climbs up then drops down and finally climbs back up to the summit of Higger Tor at 434m/1424ft. From near the summit take the right-hand of two paths, which heads over to a large boulder. At the far side of this boulder a path starts to drop downhill towards Carl Wark. Turn right at a large T-junction of tracks and ascend the summit of Carl Wark. Pass to the left of a wall of stones belonging to the fortification and turn immediate right onto a faint grassy path. In 30m scramble down some rocks off Carl Wark following a path in the direction of Burbage Bridge. After negotiating a boggy area turn left at a T-junction and then right at a fork and right at a T-junction. Bear to the right by a large boulder to reach the A625. Cross over the road onto a path opposite and make for a footbridge

Carl Walk and Higger Tor

over Burbage Brook. Turn left after the bridge and right at a T-junction. This uphill path leads back to the B6521, which you cross back over and retrace your steps first to the National Trust Visitor Centre and then to the car park.

Refreshments:	Longshaw National Trust Visitor Centre
Toilets:	Longshaw National Trust Visitor Centre
Key Features:	Carl Wark and Longshaw National Trust Visitor Centre (01433 631708)

WALK 6
Hope, Win Hill
and the Navio Roman Fort

The village of Hope nestles below the imposing silhouettes of Win Hill and Lose Hill. These hills were supposedly named after a seventh-century battle between Northumbria and Mercia, and the victors and vanquished according to legend then each camped on their respective hill.

Distance:	12km/7½ miles
Start:	Car park in Hope
Map:	OS Explorer OL1 The Peak District Dark Peak Area
Terrain:	A stiff climb towards the summit of Win Hill followed by gentle walking. The walk is a must when fair weather prevails to appreciate the magnificent views.

There was a settlement at Hope before the Normans arrived which grew into an important centre of the Royal Forest of the Peak during medieval times. Indeed the former importance of Hope, standing at the confluence of the River Noe and Peakshole Water, can be judged by the fact that it gave its name to the whole valley. The squat-spired Church of St Peter is largely fourteenth-century with the font the only remains of the original Norman affair. It contains two thirteenth-century cross slabs which are thought to carry symbols of royal forest officials or woodruffs.

Today there is very little evidence of the Navio Roman Fort except for the perimeter earthworks. The fort was strategically positioned at the confluence of the River Noe, after which it was named, and Bradwell Brook on the route of several newly constructed roads. One route ran through the Hope Valley from Chesterfield to the Melandra fort at Glossop and another road was built from Buxton to the Templeborough fort near Rotherham. The Romans invaded the Peak District in AD 78 and met very little resistance from the Brigantes.

Hope Church

They then built a handful of forts in the area, including Navio at the heart of the territory of a Brigantean tribe based at the nearby Mam Tor hill fort. It probably housed a garrison of around 500 men from the 1st Cohort of Aquitainians from southwest France and later, as with many other Roman forts, a thriving civilian community grew alongside it. It remained in use for several centuries and it is likely that its main function was to protect the Romans' lead-mining interests.

ROUTE INSTRUCTIONS

1 Turn right out of the car park and then turn left at the T-junction in 40m onto Edale Road. After several hundred metres bear right onto a No

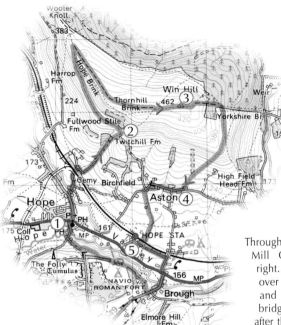

Through Road passing Mill Cottage on the right. Follow the lane over the River Noe and under a railway bridge. Immediately after the railway bridge turn right onto a track by a public footpath sign for Twitchill Farm. The track soon bends to the left and then begins a gradual climb up to the farm. The track bends to the right through the farmyard to a metal gate next to Birch Cottage. Climb steeply uphill for 75m, with ever expanding views of the Hope Valley behind you, to a public footpath sign.

2 Do not pass through the gate in front of you but turn left onto a bridleway with a plantation over to the right. Pass through a large metal gate and maintain direction along a grassy track now with fabulous views of the ridge from Lose Hill to

Mam Tor and the valley of Edale. On reaching a T-junction 75m before a plantation turn right and follow a winding track to a stile with the top of Win Hill now in sight and the Derwent Valley and the Ladybower Reservoir over to the left. Maintain direction, ignoring any offshoots, to reach Win Hill and climb off the path for several metres to the trig point at 462m/1518ft for an unbelievable 360-degree panorama.

3 Continue past the summit and begin to drop downhill to a stile. Climb the stile and at the fork in front of you bear left on the main path heading downhill into a plantation. On reaching a wall turn right by a signpost for Thornhill. Keep ahead at a marker post and then at a junction of paths turn right for Aston, passing through a gap in a wall. Follow a path across moorland, which later drops down to a stile. Continue downhill across a field to a stile. Climb the stile and walk with a wall never far away on the right to a stile and then a lane 20m further on.

4 Turn right onto Aston Lane and keep ahead at a T-junction with Parsons Lane into the hamlet of Aston. Just after a white house climb some steps on the left. Climb a stile and walk with houses on the right to reach a gate. Pass through the gate onto a surfaced driveway and then turn left on reaching Aston Lane again. In 5m climb a stile on the left, which is signposted for Hope Station, following a stream on the left. Climb a stile and negotiate a wooden squeeze stile in 10m. Climb another stile and follow the left-hand edge of three fields, ignoring the path to the left in the second field, to a kissing gate. Follow a path around to the right and over a footbridge at Hope Station to reach a lane 20m after the footbridge.

5 Turn left onto the lane and pass industrial units on the left. At a fork bear right and then turn right again in a few metres. Turn left onto the A625 and immediate right onto the B6049 opposite the Travellers Rest into Brough. Cross over the River Noe, noting a weir, and then shortly after a footbridge turn right by a public footpath sign for Hope and Castleton. Head across a field to a ladder stile to reach the site of the Navio Roman Fort. Walk across the site of the fort to a footbridge. Cross over the bridge and in the next two fields walk by a fence on the left. Maintain direction through a long field on a narrow path. Towards the end of the field the path bears to the right onto a track and soon passes between gateposts. Hope and its church come into view as you drop gently downhill to a lane. Turn right onto the lane and then turn left at a T-junction. Cross back over the River Noe and then turn left onto the A625 and return to the car park on the left.

Refreshments:	Pubs and cafes in Hope and Travellers Rest pub at Brough
Toilets:	Car park at Hope
Key Features:	The village of Hope; Win Hill; the site of Navio Roman Fort

WALK 7
Roystone Grange

Distance:	6.5km/4 miles
Start:	Minninglow car park half a mile south of Pikehall on the A5012 on a minor road between Pikehall and Parwich
Map:	OS Explorer OL24 The Peak District White Peak Area
Terrain:	Easy walking

In Derbyshire there is no evidence of affluent Roman villas complete with mosaics and central heating systems, as there is in the south of England, but there were romanised settlements based on farms or hamlets. Roystone Grange is Derbyshire's best example of such a farm.

The former owner of the present Roystone Grange, David Twigge, decided to extend his dairy in fairly recent times. It was during this work that the remains of a body were discovered, and excavations by archaeologists at Sheffield University unearthed a Roman farm and the well-preserved foundations of a medieval monastic grange run by Cistercian monks. These excavations have provided a fascinating insight into the archaeology of everyday life. More detail on the archaeology of this area can found in the Roystone Grange Trail leaflet.

Numerous quarries developed along the course of the railway, plus workings to extract high-firing silica sand and manufacture the refractory bricks in which it was used. The refractory bricks then mainly ended up in the furnaces of the Sheffield steel industry.

The 'chapel-shaped' building seen en route is in fact a nineteenth-century pump house built to send air to pneumatic drills used in the quarries on either side of the railway line. Behind the chapel is the site of the medieval grange ('grange' means a farm of monastic origins). In the reign of Henry II (1154–89) the Cistercian monks of Garendon Abbey in Leicestershire were granted this land to build a community. After the Dissolution the land was given to Rowland Babington, a distant relative of

57

Anthony Babington, ringleader of the Babington Plot.

ROUTE INSTRUCTIONS

1 Leave the car park on the High Peak Trail as signposted for High Peak Junction and immediately cross over a lane and back onto the trail. Wide-ranging views open up in front of you. The mound in the distance behind the stone embankment crowned with a clump of trees is the Neolithic or 'New Stone Age' Minninglow barrow. Follow the trail for 1.5km/1 mile, passing the post-medieval Minninglow Grange in the valley on the right and then limestone quarry workings on the left. Just after passing to the side of a gate a track called Minninglow Lane crosses the trail.

2 Turn left onto this ancient walled track with close-up views of Minninglow barrow at 372m/1220ft and climb a stile at the side of a gate. After several hundred metres and before the end of the track look out for a public footpath signpost for Roystone Grange on the right by a stile in the wall. Climb the stile and head across the middle of a field and through a tunnel under the High Peak Trail. Continue in the same direction dropping gently downhill and pass through a squeeze stile. Follow a track by a wall on the left heading towards Roystone Grange. Climb a stile in the wall and keep walking in the same direction now with the wall on the right. Pass through a squeeze stile

into a field. The 'chapel-shaped' building is over to the left. Head for a gate in the top right-hand corner of the field and join a track. Turn left if you wish to explore the pump house and the site of the grange, otherwise turn right to pass through the farm buildings of the modern Roystone Grange.

3 After passing through the farm and before reaching a cattle grid there is a disused dairy building on the left. At the back of this building are the remains of a Romano-British second-century manor house with an information board. A third/fourth-century more modest house was later built on the site of the original farm. Continue along the track and over a cattle grid. The track swings first to the left and then to the right and passes several cottages on the left.

4 At a T-junction turn left onto a surfaced stretch of Minninglow Lane and cross over Parwich Lane to continue in the same direction now on a rough track passing The Nook on the left. At a

Minninglow tumulus

public footpath sign climb a stile on the right and walk across the middle of two fields to a stile by the corner of a plantation. Climb the stile and walk diagonally across the field to a stile close to the far right-hand corner of the field. Pass through a line of trees and walk along the right-hand edge of a field. On reaching a wall corner head half right over to a stile in 20m, which returns you to the High Peak Trail. If you look over to the left you can see the bend of the Gotham Curve which turns through 80 degrees and was the tightest of any British railway line. Turn right onto the trail and return to the starting point.

Refreshments:	None
Toilets:	None
Key Features:	A section of High Peak Trail; Minninglow burial mound; Roystone Grange

WALK 8
Castleton

Distance:	9km/5½ miles
Start:	Car park in the village centre of Castleton
Map:	OS Explorer OL1 The Peak District Dark Peak Area
Terrain:	There is a gradual climb at the beginning of the walk up Cave Dale followed by easy terrain

Peveril Castle stands behind the village in a commanding position of strength on a steep limestone impregnable rocky peninsula with Cave Dale on the other side. Castleton, which takes its name from the castle, was founded as a planned medieval market town shortly after the castle was built in the twelfth century. *Ton* is an Anglo-Saxon word for enclosure. The manor incorporating the site of Peveril Castle was granted by William the Conqueror to one of his most trusted knights and his alleged illegitimate son, William Peverel, to administer the King's lead-mining and hunting interests at the centre of the Royal Forest of the Peak. By 1086, when the Domesday Book was written, a castle had been built using a combination of stone and wood, making Peveril one of the earliest stone castles.

In the gorge below Peveril Castle is the soaring entrance to Peak Cavern, which is the largest entrance to any cave in Britain. Indeed during the sixteenth and seventeenth centuries a number of cottages and an inn were based at the cave entrance. Rope makers occupied the cottages and much of their equipment is on display today at the cavern. Treak Cliff Cavern is an underground wonderland containing some of Britain's most exceptional stalactite and stalagmite formations and the

The village of Castleton, set at the very heart of the Peak District, is known as the 'Gem of the Peaks'. It has a spectacular location at the head of the Hope Valley surrounded by hills, including the moody Mam Tor, at the geological junction of the White and Dark Peak. The imposing ruins of Peveril Castle sit on the hillside above the village, and there are four show caves, an ancient late Bronze Age/early Iron Age fort and a wealth of other historical interest in the immediate locality. Castleton's dazzling array of natural and historical features above and below ground mean that today the village is a tourist honeypot. Every year Castleton celebrates Garland Day (see Introduction).

Castleton

famous translucent semi-precious Blue John mineral stone. Castleton is the only place in the world where Blue John occurs naturally, and its beauty has been prized since Roman times for ornaments and jewellery. It is a colour-banded form of fluorspar which is thought to take its name from the French *bleu et jaune*, the 'blue and yellow' stone. The use of the mineral stone is found far and wide today including, for example, in the Vatican and the White House. Blue John is still commercially mined from Treak Cliff at a rate of half a ton per year. Blue John Cavern itself contained the first Blue John workings but the veins have now been fully exploited. The final show cave stands at the foot of Winnats Pass and is reached by a unique journey on a boat along an underground 'canal'. Two hundred years ago lead miners using primitive hand tools dug out this tunnel to create a route to a huge natural complex of underground streams and caverns. Speedwell Cavern, however, had only a short life as it was opened in 1771 after a £14,000 investment and then closed in 1790 after only £3000 worth of iron ore had been extracted.

Opposite Peveril Castle and Castleton is the dramatic landmark of Mam Tor. (For information on Mam Tor see Walk 4.) The Odin Mine, at the foot of Mam Tor, is the earliest identifiable lead mine in Derbyshire, which was recorded in 1280.

ROUTE INSTRUCTIONS

1 Turn left out of the car park onto the A625 and turn right along Castle Street passing the Church of St Edmund on the left. Bear left at a junction into the Market Place passing the village green. In 30m turn right by a public footpath signpost by Cavedale Cottage and soon climb a stile by the side of a gate into Cave Dale, a spectacular limestone gorge. The rocky path heads uphill but it is worth stopping for frequent breaks and turning around for a view of the keep of Peveril Castle perched up on the cliff top. Pass through a gate and follow the path on much gentler ground with a wall on the right. After negotiating a metal gate

Mam Tor

63

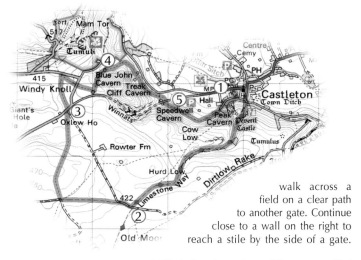

walk across a field on a clear path to another gate. Continue close to a wall on the right to reach a stile by the side of a gate.

2 Climb the stile and turn right onto a walled track after climbing another stile. At a junction climb the stile in front of you to walk along a track on the left-hand edge of a field by a wall. Pass through a gap at the side of a gate and maintain direction in the next field. At a junction of paths climb a stile on the right to follow the left-hand edge of a field by a wall. Continue towards Mam Tor crossing two stiles and then follow a grassy downhill path to the B6061.

3 Cross over the road and turn right. In a few metres climb a stile on the left and walk initially with a wall on the left continuing towards Mam Tor. Fifty metres before a gate onto the A625 there is T-junction, which you ignore, but at the next T-junction 20m from the gate turn right and follow the path to the B6061. Cross over the road to the stile opposite, which is signposted for Winnats Head Farm. Walk across the middle of a field to a

Peveril Castle from Cave Dale

stile. Fifty metres after the stile turn left at a public footpath sign for Blue John Cavern. There is no path on the ground but the route is easy to follow as you head towards the old Mam Tor road, which was closed following landslides on the Shivering Mountain, for 75m and then bear to the right and downhill to the Blue John Cavern.

4 Climb a large stile to the right of the cavern into a field and follow it to another stile, with good views of the side of Mam Tor, which has suffered landslides. The path then continues around a hill to Treak Cliff Cavern. Castleton comes into view and the ore-crushing circle of the Odin Mine can also be seen in the valley bottom below just to the far side of the closed Mam Tor road. Leave the cavern by the steps down to the Mam Tor road but 40m before you reach the road bear right onto a grassy path towards the flag of Speedwell Cavern at the foot of the spectacular Winnats Pass. At a fork keep left by a wall to a stile and head for another stile in 100m just to the left of the cavern.

*Win Hill from the top
of Winnats Pass*

5 Cross over the road and pass through a gate onto the Longcliff Estate to walk with a wall on the left. Climb a stile at the side of a gate and at a fork ignore the higher-level route and continue next to the wall to reach a gate. Pass through a gate to join a track walled on both sides, which soon leads to a surfaced lane. At a T-junction turn right to admire the cottages of Castleton. At the next junction it is worth turning right to obtain a close-up view of the massive entrance to the Peak Cavern in 75m; otherwise turn left to walk along Peak's Hole Water and then cross a bridge on the right. Take the next left by the Carlton Emporium to keep by the water's edge and return to the A625 opposite the car park.

Refreshments:	Pubs and cafes in Castleton and cafes at Blue John Cavern and Treak Cliff Cavern
Toilets:	Car park at Castleton
Key Features:	The village of Castleton, including Peveril Castle (01433 620613) and its four show caves (Treak Cliff cavern – 01433 620571, Blue John Cavern – 01433 620638, Speedwell Cavern – 01433 620512 and Peak Cavern – 01433 620285); Mam Tor; the Odin Mine

WALK 9
Hartington and Pilsbury Castle

Distance:	8km/5 miles
Start:	Hartington Market Place on the B5054
Map:	OS Explorer OL24 The Peak District White Peak Area
Terrain:	Other than one climb after visiting the site of Pilsbury Castle this walk is along a flat gated road plus field walking

During the 1870s the Duke of Devonshire established a creamery at Hartington. Later in the 1920s and 1930s the creamery held a Royal Warrant to supply cheese to George V. Again during the 1920s the creamery began to make stilton, for example, Buxton Blue and White Stilton and a more recent cheese called Dovedale. Today it is one of a few cheese factories in the country allowed to make blue-veined stilton, the 'King of English Cheeses', and it sells its produce in Ye Olde Cheese Shoppe in the Market Place.

Hartington Hall, which stands near the village centre, is a fine stone mullioned manor house built in 1611 and was occupied by the Bateman family until it became a youth hostel in 1934. It is alleged that Bonnie Prince Charlie slept at the hall on 3 December 1745 on his abortive march to London.

Pilsbury Castle, an early Norman motte and bailey castle, probably situated on the site of an Iron Age fort, is located in a quiet but scenic stretch of the Upper Dove Valley. Today all that remains is a mound of the earthworks, as the wooden structure was never replaced by stone. The castle was built at the centre of the De Ferrers estate, suggesting that it was an important administrative centre until the function was transferred to Hartington.

Hartington is one of the Peak District's bustling tourist honeypots. It was once an important and prosperous market town, as reflected in the limestone cottages, former coaching inns and shops ringing the spacious Market Place, along with its duckpond. Although it is a long time since a market was held in Hartington a market charter was granted as early as 1203. The hilltop and imposing Parish Church of St Giles, which is mainly thirteenth and fourteenth century, also reflects the early importance of the town. Interestingly the title of Marquis of Hartington is a secondary title of the Dukes of Devonshire granted as a courtesy title to the eldest son and heir.

The castle ceased to be used by the fourteenth century. There is an information board at the site providing further details of this Norman castle.

ROUTE INSTRUCTIONS

1 From the Market Place at Hartington follow Dig Street, which is signposted for Pilsbury and soon becomes a gated road. After the last of the houses of Hartington continue for 4km/2½ miles to the hamlet of Pilsbury through the Upper Dove Valley. Along the route first pass Bank Top Farm then the entrance to Sprink Farm, Ludwell Farm and Parks Barn to finally reach a farmhouse at Pilsbury. There are views of Chrome Hill in the distance, and as you approach Pilsbury the gritstone peak of Sheen Hill stands on the left. The seventeenth-century Broadmeadow Hall can also be seen over to the left close to Pilsbury. Shortly after the farmhouse the road bends sharply to the right. Keep ahead onto a track and follow it to the mound of Pilsbury Castle in several hundred metres.

2 Retrace your steps to the lane and pass the farmhouse again in the hamlet. A few metres after the farmhouse pass through a gate and turn right onto a track with a wall on the right to a footbridge over the River Dove. Turn right after the footbridge to walk uphill on a track. In 100m pass through a gate on the left into a field by a footpath sign for Sheen. Walk diagonally across a large field heading up towards a broken line of trees to a gate in a wall by a marker

post. Head half right in the next field to a wall and turn left to walk with the wall on your right for 75m. Turn right through a squeeze stile and bear half left to walk between two gateposts. Head across a field to a gap in a wall and follow the right-hand edge of a field for 40m to a public footpath sign. Turn right through a gap and follow the path across a field to a stile. Climb the stile onto a track and turn right to reach a lane in a few metres.

3 Turn left onto the lane and in 100m, when the lane bends to the right, bear left into Harris Close Farm. Do not walk through the farm but keep by the wall on the right for 15m to a stile next to a barn. Follow the right-hand edge of three fields at which point Hartington and its cheese factory come into view. Again in the next field walk along the right-hand edge and then maintain direction towards a conifer plantation. A path runs close to the edge of the plantation to a stile at the far end. Climb the stile and follow a path which bears to the left and drops steeply downhill to a stile. Climb the stile onto a track and turn right. In 75m by a public footpath sign turn left through a gate. Walk across the middle of a field and cross a footbridge over the River Dove. Bear right after the footbridge and follow a path negotiating stiles to reach the cheese factory by a lane. Turn left onto the lane and return to the Market Place.

Refreshments:	Pubs and cafes in Hartington
Toilets:	Hartington
Key Features:	The village of Hartington; a stretch of the upper Dove Valley; the earthworks of Pilsbury Castle

The area of Dale Abbey is named after a now ruined abbey founded around 1160 and dissolved in 1538. Essentially all that remains of St Mary's Abbey is the east window arch. If you wish to visit the ruins permission must be sought from the owners at Abbey House.

Distance:	7km/4½ miles
Start:	Roadside parking on the No Through Road opposite the Carpenter's Arms at Dale Abbey approached from either junction 25 of the M1 or the A6096
Map:	OS Explorer 260 Nottingham
Terrain:	A flat gentle walk across fields and through parkland

The history of Dale Abbey can be traced back to around 1130 when Cornelius, a baker from Derby, allegedly had a vision instructing him to go to what was then known as Depedale to worship God. He carved out for himself a cave in a sandstone cliff which can be visited by a short detour from the route instructions. The Hermitage is a Scheduled Ancient Monument and has a particularly well-preserved door and two windows. Word spread that this was an area of religious importance and an abbey was founded here, along with the Church of All Saints around 1150. This church is one of the smallest and strangest in the country. The building itself is part church and part house, and in the nineteenth century the latter used to be a pub. Inside the church the pulpit, reading desk and clerk's pew are all behind the altar, and this is a rare example of an arrangement still found in a church that is still in use.

Smith of Warwick built Locko Hall in the late 1720s and once complete in 1747 it was sold to the Drury-Lowes and has remained the seat of this family ever since. Various additions were made to the hall through-out the course of the nineteenth century. The Italian influences of the great Victorian traveller and collector William Drury-Lowe can clearly be seen. Locko Park, surrounding the hall, comprises 3000 acres of agricultural estate land and 600 acres of parkland. Please keep to the well-marked footpaths through the estate as this is all private property.

ROUTE INSTRUCTIONS

1 Walk along the No Through Road away from the Carpenter's Arms and pass a church on the right. At a junction turn right onto Tattle Hill. At the end of the lane climb a stile by the side of a gate. Ignore the track and bear to the right along the edge of a field to a stile in 30m. Climb the stile and turn left at a T-junction of paths. Climb a stile and head across the middle of a field to another stile. Follow the right-hand edge of a field to join a grassy track which leads to the A6096.

2 Turn left onto the main road and at the end of the buildings of Flourish Farm turn right onto a surfaced driveway signposted to Hollies Farm. Follow the driveway between the buildings of Hollies Farm to reach a gate. Pass through the gate and walk along a gravel track to a T-junction in 50m. Climb the stile in front of you into a field.

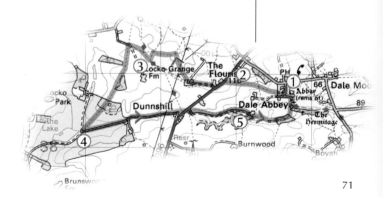

Walk across two fields via a stile and climb another stile to follow the left-hand edge of a field. At a crossroad of paths by a footpath sign climb a stile and then another immediately on the left. Head across the middle of a field to a stile and then half right to cross two stiles in quick succession. Turn left to climb another two stiles within 100m and maintain direction to reach a grassy track 30m further on.

3 Turn right onto the track and follow the left-hand edge of fields to a gate. Bear to the left along the field edge and pass through a gate onto a track. Turn left through a large metal gate towards Locko Grange Farm, but immediately leave the track to walk along the right-hand edge of fields. After climbing the third stile turn left along the field edge to a stile. Head across the next field with a young plantation on the left to a footbridge. The top of a tower of Locko Hall can be seen over to the right. Walk along the left-hand edge of the next field towards woodland. Enter the woodland via a metal kissing gate and follow the clear path through it. On emerging from the trees maintain direction across Locko Park to reach a junction of surfaced driveways through the park.

4 Turn left and when the surfaced driveway ends at East Lodge continue ahead, ignoring the track off to the right just after the lodge, along a rough track to reach the A6096. Cross over the road with care to the footpath opposite by a public footpath sign. Walk through trees to a T-junction and turn right onto a track which leads to Columbine Farm.

5 In front of the farm bear to the right along a track to reach a gate in 75m. Pass through the gate and follow the left-hand edge of a field which leads into an area known as Dale Hills. Enter

Ockbrook Wood via a gate and follow the track along the edge of the wood. After emerging from the wood the path gradually bends to the left to a gate. Glimpses of the ruins of St Mary's Abbey can be seen. At a T-junction of paths in front of a house turn left to pass the tiny All Saint's Church, part church and part house. A short detour can be taken here to visit the Hermitage, otherwise continue past Abbey House and turn right at the junction to return to the starting point.

Refreshments:	The Carpenter's Arms at Dale
Toilets:	None
Key Features:	The village of Dale Abbey and Locko Hall and its park

WALK 11
Chelmorton

Chelmorton is one of the highest villages in England and is a nationally famous historic landscape. The village is based on one street lined with cottages. Allotted to each cottage are strip fields, which have been perfectly preserved since medieval times relating to the first enclosure of land. These ancient fields were then 'fossilised' by the drystone walls of the eighteenth-century Enclosure Movement.

Distance:	7km/4½ miles
Start:	Wye Dale car park on the A6 opposite Topley Pike Quarry, which is 6.5km/4 miles east of Buxton
Map:	OS Explorer OL24 The Peak District White Peak Area
Terrain:	Although not a long walk there is a short steep climb out of a valley at the beginning of the walk. More importantly the climb back down into this valley towards the end of the walk is steep and there is a 20m stretch on a potentially vertiginous and unfenced narrow ledge by Topley Pike Quarry. Please do not take young children and dogs without a lead on this walk.

The oldest part of Chelmorton village is centred on the partly thirteenth-century Parish Church of St John the Baptist, topped with a locust weather vane, and an inn containing some twelfth-century stone. This end of the village is guarded over by Chelmorton Low on which there are two Bronze Age tumuli. A stream runs off Chelmorton Low, curiously named Illy Willy Stream, and runs down through the centre of 'Chelly' as the locals refer to it. The network of green lanes surrounding the village, some of which are followed on this walk, relate to the medieval access lanes which ran between the strips of land.

ROUTE INSTRUCTIONS

1 From the car park cross over the A6 with extreme care to the entrance to Topley Pike Quarry. Just to the left of the driveway there is a public footpath which runs alongside the quarry up into a valley. At a footpath sign keep ahead along the valley bottom for Chelmorton. When you reach what looks like a dead end by a churn hole, bear to the right and climb steeply up and out of the valley to a stile. Climb the stile and bear to the left along a field edge with a wall on the left. In the next field head over to a track and follow this towards Burrs Farm, passing Chelmorton Flat over to the left. When the track bends to the left at the end of the field bear slightly to the right to a stile. Pass Burrs Farm and maintain direction to a stile at the side of gate to join a green lane with Chelmorton Low standing prominent over to the left. Follow this track to the A5270 and cross over the road to the green lane opposite. This lane leads to Chelmorton which can be clearly seen ahead, passing Shepley Farm along the route.

2 When you reach the cottages of Chelmorton it is worth briefly turning left for a close-up view of the church and perhaps also the inn! Retrace your steps and follow the one and only street through the village. Ignore the road on the right and then 75m further on turn right by a public footpath sign. When you reach Ollershaw Farm negotiate a small gate in front of you which leads to a stile into field in 20m. Walk along the right-hand edge of the field to a stile and then along the left-hand edge of the next field. Climb a stile onto a green lane and turn left. Follow the lane as it bends to the right and keep ahead at a T-junction to reach the A5270.

3 Cross over to the green lane opposite and follow this as it gradually bends to the right. Keep ahead at a marker post when a path crosses the track and then at a T-junction of green lanes 30m further on turn left. Just before this green lane ends with a gate in front of you climb a stile on the right into a field. Walk half left roughly following the line of telegraph wires to a stile with Topley Quarry down below. At this point exercise extreme care because after climbing the stile you turn right for 20m along a very narrow unfenced ledge. The path looks as though it ends and that you are about to fall off the edge but if you carefully inch forward you will see a clear path, which drops very steeply down to the valley bottom. Turn right in the bottom at a T-junction of paths and then left at the next T-junction to retrace your steps through the valley to the A6. Again take care when crossing this road.

Refreshments:	The Church Inn at Chelmorton
Toilets:	None
Key Features:	The historic landscape of Chelmorton

WALK 12
Hartington and Beresford
and Wolfscote Dales

Distance:	13km/8 miles
Start:	Hartington Market Place on the B5054
Map:	OS Explorer OL24 The Peak District White Peak Area
Terrain:	This is very pleasant walking country, although there is a steep descent from Gipsy Bank to the banks of the River Dove in Wolfscote Dale

Alstonefield is a peaceful and unspoilt village located just over the border in Staffordshire, which stands on a limestone plateau between the Dove and Manifold valleys. Its grey stone cottages are grouped around a charming green and village inn which is popular with walkers.

Alstonefield lies at the crossroads of several old packhorse routes and once had its own market created by charter in 1308, although the market ceased in 1500. The church is reached from a lane leading off from the green. It is mainly fourteenth and fifteenth century, but it does contain a Norman doorway and chancel arch and it has an elaborate pew dedicated to the local Cotton family.

It was on a stretch of water in Beresford Dale that Izaak Walton and his friend Charles Cotton from the nearby Beresford Hall used their trout fishing adventures and experiences to write *The Compleat Angler* which was published in 1653. Beresford Hall has now been demolished and all that remains is an ornate fishing temple once used by Walton and Cotton. Pike Pool was named by Charles Cotton, not after the fish but after the tall spire of rock which stands above the river there.

Information about Hartington can be found under Walk 9.

ROUTE INSTRUCTIONS

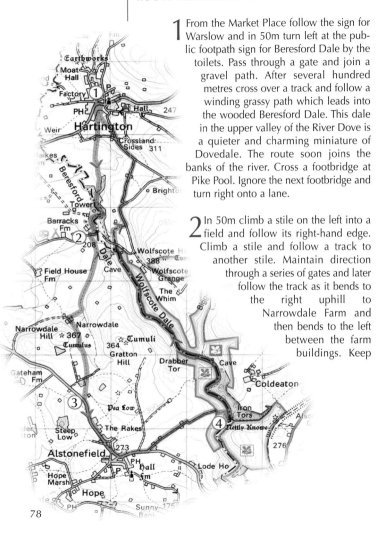

1 From the Market Place follow the sign for Warslow and in 50m turn left at the public footpath sign for Beresford Dale by the toilets. Pass through a gate and join a gravel path. After several hundred metres cross over a track and follow a winding grassy path which leads into the wooded Beresford Dale. This dale in the upper valley of the River Dove is a quieter and charming miniature of Dovedale. The route soon joins the banks of the river. Cross a footbridge at Pike Pool. Ignore the next footbridge and turn right onto a lane.

2 In 50m climb a stile on the left into a field and follow its right-hand edge. Climb a stile and follow a track to another stile. Maintain direction through a series of gates and later follow the track as it bends to the right uphill to Narrowdale Farm and then bends to the left between the farm buildings. Keep

Hartington Church

ahead to enter what is initially a narrow field walled on both sides. On reaching a stile in the wall on the left ignore the stile and follow the path as it bends to the right away from the wall and climbs up to a stile. Walk along the right-hand edge of the next field and pass through a squeeze stile in a field corner. Head across the middle of two fields and cross over a track. The route then heads half right across the next field to a gate. At the far side of yet another field, pass through a squeeze stile by the side of a gate and then make for a stile onto a lane.

3 Turn left onto the lane and follow it into the village of Alstonefield. Bear left at a sign for Ashbourne to pass a parking area and toilets on the right to reach the lovely village green. Continue ahead at another sign for Ashbourne and take the second public footpath sign on the left onto a track, which initially has a high wall on the right. This is essentially a straight track apart from a sharp right-hand bend quickly followed by sharp left-hand bend just after the halfway point which

leads to the top of Gipsy Bank with the River Dove below. Climb a stile onto the bank and bear to the right by a National Trust sign to begin the long and very steep descent to the footbridge seen from the top over the river.

4 Cross over the footbridge and turn left to follow a marvellous route through Wolfscote Dale for several miles beside limestone cliffs and crags. At the next footbridge by a National Trust sign leave the riverbank and turn half right along an uphill track. When the track bends to the right after 50m keep ahead and continue uphill and follow it around the next right-hand bend to a lane. Turn left onto the lane and just after a right-hand bend turn left onto a track which is signposted for Hartington. The track soon bends to the right and then continues in a straight line to a lane. Turn left onto the lane and when it bends to the right with a magnificent view of the church at Hartington pass through a squeeze stile in front of you to soon follow the right-hand edge of a field dropping downhill towards Hartington. At a wall corner turn right and pass through a gate onto a road. Turn left and left again to return to the Market Place.

Refreshments:	Pubs and cafes at Hartington and Alstonefield
Toilets:	Hartington and Alstonefield
Key Features:	The villages of Hartington and Alstonefield, and Beresford and Wolfscote Dales along the River Dove

WALK 13
Tideswell

Distance:	8km/5 miles
Start:	Roadside parking in Tideswell near the church or alternatively Tideswell Dale car park on the B6049 between Tideswell and Miller's Dale
Map:	OS Explorer OL24 The Peak District White Peak Area
Terrain:	Pleasant and easygoing field and trail walking

During the early medieval period Tideswell was an important royal centre on the southern edge of the Royal Forest of the Peak. It was granted a market charter in 1250 and flourished under the wool and lead trades during the fourteenth century, which explains how it came to have such a large and magnificent church for a small village. St John the Baptist's Church is known as 'the Cathedral of the Peak' and it took 75 years of hard work to complete with a short cessation of work during 1349–50 due to the plague.

The church at Tideswell is built in the Decorated style, but due to the length of time it took to complete the work the tower is in the Perpendicular style, which by that time was the architectural fashion. The church is Tidewell's main tourist attraction, but the long village set along a main street with numerous alleyways is well worth exploring.

ROUTE INSTRUCTIONS

1 From the church walk into the village of Tideswell along the main street. Opposite the Nat West Bank turn right onto Parke Road. Turn left at a T-junction by the United Reformed Church and at the second public footpath sign on the right attached to a telegraph pole pass through a gap at the side of a gate. Follow the right-hand edge of three fields and turn left onto a track called Slancote Lane. When the track bends to the left maintain direction and climb a stile into a field.

'Cathedral of the Peak', Tideswell

Walk across the middle of the field to a wall corner and climb a stile, which is 5m beyond it. Follow the left-hand edge of a field and turn left onto a track to join the Limestone Way.

2 The track bends to the left to a T-junction where you turn right and drop gently down to a stile by the side of a gate. The track later bends to the left to reach a gate at the side of a farm. Thirty metres beyond the gate turn right at a signpost for the Limestone Way and bear right again in a few metres as signposted. Pass through a gate and continue downhill into the valley bottom. Turn right on reaching a lane and keep ahead onto the B6049 in Miller's Dale. Opposite the church take the lane for Litton Mill, immediately passing Miller's Dale Meal Mill and its waterwheel. A few metres after the mill turn right to cross a footbridge over the River Wye. Bear to the left as signposted for the Monsal Trail and Priestcliffe and climb up through woodland to reach the Monsal Trail.

3 Turn left onto the trail and follow it for 2km. After passing under a railway bridge the trail bears to the left at a signpost for Litton Mill

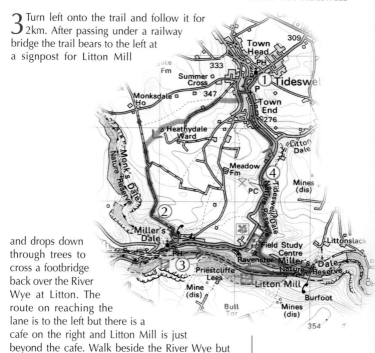

and drops down through trees to cross a footbridge back over the River Wye at Litton. The route on reaching the lane is to the left but there is a cafe on the right and Litton Mill is just beyond the cafe. Walk beside the River Wye but just after a Field Study Centre sign bear to the right along a track by a crag and signpost for Tideswell Dale. Bear to the right over a footbridge in the dale and then turn immediate left ignoring the concessionary footpath ahead. Keep ahead at a junction to reach a gate. Continue along a surfaced path to reach Tideswell Dale car park.

4 Just before reaching the road there is a signpost on the right for Tideswell village. The path soon reaches the B6049. Cross over to the pavement at the other side and turn right. Just after passing a sewage treatment works turn left by a public footpath sign. The path climbs up into a

83

Wood carving in Tideswell Dale

field and soon bends to the right to head through trees and later walking with a wire fence on the right to reach a gate on the left. Pass through the gate and continue along a track towards Tideswell. Turn right at a T-junction with a road and drop down to the B6049. Turn left to walk through the village back to the church.

Refreshments:	Pubs and cafes in Tideswell and a cafe at Litton
Toilets:	Tideswell and Tideswell Dale car park
Key Features:	The village of Tideswell and its 'Cathedral of the Peak'; a section of the Monsal Trail; Litton and Tideswell Dale

WALK 14
Ashbourne

Distance:	9km/5½ miles
Start:	Tissington Trail cycle hire centre on Mapleton Road, which is sign-posted from near the Market Place in Ashbourne
Map:	OS Explorer 259 Derby
Terrain:	Easy field and trail walking

Ashbourne is the southern gateway to the Peak District and at one time was an important town on the Manchester to London coach route, having at that time a larger population than Derby. When the railways came to Ashbourne, however, it was only as a branch line, and the town therefore did not develop greatly during the Victorian age despite its summer tourist trade. This lack of nineteenth-century development has meant that a rare combination of a medieval street plan and Georgian façade architecture has been preserved. Indeed St John's Street has been described as 'architecturally the best in Derbyshire' with its famous Ashbourne Gingerbread shop and a gallows-style Green Man Inn sign stretched across the street. During the twentieth century a new town grew up around the old market town.

ROUTE INSTRUCTIONS

1 From the cycle hire centre at one end of the Tissington Trail join the trail as it heads towards Parsley Hay at the far end. The trail soon drops down to a river and then climbs back up to a gate. After the gate there are two footpath signs on the left. Ignore the first one and continue on for 20m to climb a stile into a field. Turn right to walk along the field edge towards a farm parallel to the trail,

Ashbourne is a popular tourist destination and becomes a hive of activity on market days. The town is also the home of Derwent Crystal. Where Church Street joins on to St John's Street you will find the magnificent mainly early thir-teenth-century Church of St Oswald with its graceful 65m/212ft spire reflecting Ash-bourne's prosperous past. Ashbourne became Oakbourne in the book *Adam Bede* by George Eliot. See the Introduction for details of Ashbourne's Shrovetide football game.

but towards the end of the field head half left over to a stile by the side of a gate. Turn left onto a surfaced lane to walk next to a stream. When the lane bends to the left to Callow Top Farm climb a stile on the right into a field.

2 Turn right to walk along the right-hand edge of two fields. Maintain direction across the middle of four fields, then the right-hand edge of the next field before heading across the middle of another field. The next field is longer and you walk close to its left-hand edge with Hinchley Wood on the left. Climb a stile at the end of the field at a corner of the wood and bear to the left to a squeeze stile in 10m. Turn right to walk along the right-hand edge of two fields with the prominent shape of Thorpe Cloud looming in front of you. Head across a field keeping to the left of a

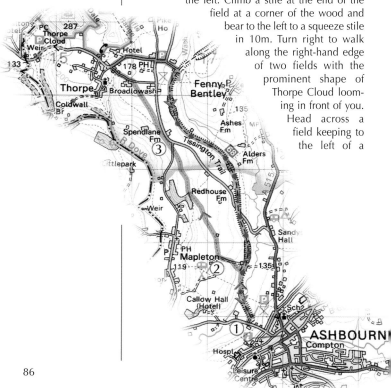

field corner and then walk over to another field corner and maintain direction so that you are walking with a hedge on the right to reach a lane.

3 Turn right onto the lane and then climb a stile in 15m on the left by a public footpath sign into a field. Pass through a gate in 10m and walk close to the right-hand edge of a field. When you are opposite Spendlane Farm move slightly over to the left heading for a gap by a public footpath sign 10m to the right of gate. Head across this long field to a gate and signpost for Thorpe close to a corner of the field. Pass through a gap at the side of the gate and walk diagonally across the field to a stile onto a lane by the side of a barn. Turn left onto the lane and walk downhill to a T-junction in Thorpe. Here turn right to pass the Peveril of the Peak on the left. At a junction by the Dog and Partridge pub cross over to take the lane opposite which is sign-posted for Tissington with Narlows car park on the left. Just before the lane bends to the left bear to the right and walk to another car park by the side of the Tissington Trail. From the car park turn right onto the Tissington Trail. At the end of the car park there is a sign 'Ashbourne 2 miles'. Follow the trail back to the cycle hire centre.

Refreshments:	Tissington Trail cycle hire centre and the Dog and Partridge pub near Thorpe
Toilets:	Tissington Trail cycle hire centre
Key Features:	A section of the Tissington Trail and the opportunity to explore Ashbourne separately from the route of the walk

WALK 15
Bakewell and Ashford in the Water

Today tourism is very much Bakewell's economic mainstay and this pretty, attractive market town provides an excellent base for touring the Peak District. A number of traditions are also maintained in Bakewell, such as the annual well dressing (see Introduction) and the Bakewell Show held in August. This is one of the largest and most popular agricultural shows in the country.

Distance:	12km/7½ miles
Start:	The long-stay car park near town bridge. Just before the town bridge approaching Bakewell on the A619 turn left onto Station Road and right in a few metres onto Coombs Road.
Map:	OS Explorer OL24 The Peak District White Peak Area
Terrain:	A gentle walk along lanes, a trail and fields

Bakewell is a small stone-built town on the River Wye and is generally regarded as the capital of the Peak District. Indeed the headquarters of the Peak District National Park is located on the edge of the town. The earliest known fact about the area is that an Iron Age fort was built on a hill near Ball Cross but Bakewell, meaning 'Badeca's spring' or 'well', began to grow in Saxon times. The manor came under the control of William Peverel after the Norman Conquest. A small motte and bailey castle was built just across the town bridge on Castle Hill to guard the crossing. Subsequently Bakewell came under the control of the Dukes of Rutland from nearby Haddon Hall.

Bakewell has played various roles during its long history, first as an important route and trade centre. Bakewell's market town status was confirmed by charter in 1330 and a cattle market is still held every Monday. The Duke of Rutland attempted to create Bakewell as a spa town around 1700 but this was not successful because, unlike Buxton and Matlock, the water was comparatively cold. The Bath House that the duke built in 1697 survives today but is not open to the public.

Bakewell has also acted as a minor textile centre, and Richard Arkwright sited one of his mills on the River Wye close to Bakewell.

The Parish Church of All Saints stands in an elevated position dominating the view for miles around. The church dates back to Norman times with additions over the next few centuries, but it was substantially rebuilt in the mid-nineteenth century. It contains many interesting features including two ninth-century Saxon crosses and various Saxon carvings. There is also a monument to Dorothy Vernon and John Manners who, according to romantic legend, eloped from Haddon Hall. The early importance of Bakewell can be identified from the *Domesday Book*, when it was recorded as one of the few places in Derbyshire to have two priests and a church.

Bakewell is probably best known for its culinary accident by the cook at the Rutland Arms, birthplace of the Bakewell pudding. The Rutland Arms, or the White Horse Inn as it then was, was built in 1804 as a coaching inn. Around 1860 the cook was asked to make a strawberry jam tart for some important guests but the jam was put in first and the egg mixture poured in afterwards, instead of the other way round. The result, however, proved to be an instant hit, but be warned: never refer to Bakewell pudding as Bakewell tart in Bakewell! Jane Austen once stayed at the Rutland Arms and used it as a setting in her novel *Pride and Prejudice*.

Ashford in the Water is situated on the ancient Portway packhorse route and was once an important crossing on the River Wye. Its name literally means 'a ford near ash trees'. The village consists of a delightful jumble of mainly eighteenth- and nineteenth-century limestone cottages. Its most famous landmark is the much-photographed seventeenth-century Sheepwash Bridge, including its small sheepfold, and the village still practises the custom of well dressing. The parish church has a Norman tympanum from the original church and the base of the tower is thirteenth century but the rest was largely rebuilt around 1870. Hanging from the roof of the church are four paper decorated garlands or

Ashford in the Water

virgins' crants or crowns. In line with a tradition previously widespread across England, these garlands were carried at the funeral processions of unmarried girls and then hung from the church roof in their memory. It is unusual, however, to find any surviving garlands of this tradition. Another feature in the church are the memorials made from Ashford black marble, a locally quarried limestone which took on a black appearance when polished. Its production ceased in 1905 but it was in great demand by the Victorians for objets d'art.

The Monsal Trail runs along the trackbed of part of the former Midland Railway line which linked London and Manchester in the 1860s. The line had reached Rowsley near Chatsworth by 1849, but both the Duke of Devonshire at Chatsworth and the Duke of Rutland at Haddon Hall refused to allow a railway line to run through their estates. Eventually the Duke of Rutland permitted the railway company, at great expense, to build a tunnel under the Haddon Estate and the line was extended to Buxton by 1863. A personal station was erected for the Duke of Rutland at Bakewell and likewise a station was built for the Duke of Devonshire at Hassop. The railway was closed in 1968 and a section was later purchased by the Peak District National Park and converted into a trail. The Monsal Trail runs for 13.5km/8½ miles southeast of Bakewell from Coombes Viaduct to the Blackwell Mill junction near Buxton following the deep valley of the River Wye.

ROUTE INSTRUCTIONS

1 From the parking area turn right onto Coombs Road and follow it for 1.5km/1 mile to a railway viaduct. As you leave Bakewell the controversial and modern Agricultural and Business Centre where the livestock market takes place can be seen on the right. Just before the viaduct bear left onto a track signposted for the Monsal Trail and at a T-junction turn left to join the trail at its southeastern end. There are good views of Bakewell and its church as the trail heads back towards Bakewell

Haddon Hall, Walk 16

91

and passes the former railway station. Continue on and under the A619 and then pass the Country Book Store in the former Hassop railway station on your left by the next road. Pass above the A6020 and, on reaching a former railway station, leave the Monsal Trail by climbing some steps on the right up to a bridge.

2 Turn right onto a lane and soon walk past Thornbridge Education Centre. Turn around at the entrance for a view of Thornbridge Hall which now acts as the centre. Follow the lane downhill and turn left through a squeeze stile at a signpost for Ashford into a field. Walk along the left-hand edge of a field and pass first through a gate and then a squeeze stile. Negotiate another squeeze stile by the side of a

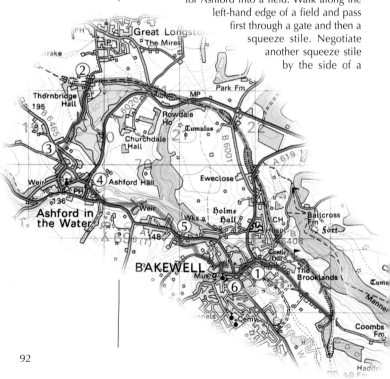

barn and soon cross over a lane and pass through a gate and into a small field. Cross the middle of the field and turn left onto Vicarage Lane which drops down into Ashford in the Water.

Sheepwash Bridge, Ashford in the Water

3 At a junction with a grassy area continue ahead. The route passes around a sharp left-hand bend but before negotiating this bend maintain direction for a few metres onto Sheepwash Bridge. It is worth crossing the former packhorse bridge and turning left for a full view of the bridge and its sheepfold before retracing your steps and turning right on the bend. The custom of washing sheep each year in the water by the bridge is still maintained today.

4 Pass the Holy Trinity Parish Church of Ashford on the left and various pubs on Church Street until you reach the A6020. Cross over this road with care onto a lane with a No Entry to Vehicles sign, passing Ashford Cricket Club on the left. Cross a bridge over the River Wye and turn left

Haddon Hall, Walk 16

onto a footpath just before reaching the A6. In 40m turn left through a gate by a public footpath sign and follow marker posts across meadows with the River Wye on the left to pass through two gates in quick succession opposite two weirs. Cross a stile and follow a grassy path as it bends to the right towards housing. Climb a stile in front of a house and continue to a lane. Cross over the lane and continue ahead to climb a stile into a field. At the other side of the field pass through a gap at the side of a gate onto the A6.

5 Turn left onto the road for 40m and then cross to the other side to join a path that climbs steeply uphill into woodland. The path then bends to the left and emerges onto a sports field. Follow the right-hand edge of the sports field and walk across a car park to a road. Turn left onto the lane, which bends first to the left and then to the right. At a fork bear left to pass the church on your right. At a T-junction turn right to pass the Rutland Arms Hotel and cross over a road.

6 In 20m turn left onto a pedestrian crossing on Matlock Street. Turn left at the other side of the road and follow the footpath round to the right, passing the Old Original Bakewell Pudding Shop and the Queens Arms. The Old Original Bakewell Pudding Shop and two other shops in Bakewell all claim to hold the original secret recipe and continue today to export their puddings all over the world. Pass the National Park Information Centre on the right which is based in the former Market Hall built in the seventeenth century. Cross over the town bridge and turn right onto Station Road and right again onto Coombs Road to return to the starting point. Town Bridge is a beautiful medieval five-arched bridge and is one of the oldest in the country.

Refreshments:	Pubs and cafes in Bakewell and Ashford in the Water
Toilets:	Bakewell and Ashford in the Water
Key Features:	Bakewell; a section of the Monsal Trail; Ashford in the Water

Built on top of a limestone crop overlooking the River Wye is the romantic medieval manor house of Haddon Hall, a relic from the Age of Chivalry, surrounded by its award winning rose gardens. This wonderful example of a non-fortified medieval house, a sleeping beauty, was given the kiss of life in the 1920s when the father of the current Duke of Rutland began a period of restoration. Haddon Hall has belonged to the direct descendants of the present duke for over 800 years.

Distance:	11.5km/7 miles
Start:	The long-stay car park near the town bridge. Just before the town bridge, approaching Bakewell on the A619, turn left onto Station Road and right in a few metres onto Coombs Road.
Map:	OS Explorer OL24 The Peak District White Peak Area
Terrain:	There is a gentle uphill section along Intake Lane with a steeper climb after leaving the Wye later on. The path from Haddon Hall back to Bakewell can become a little overgrown with nettles in the summer.

Haddon Hall with its turrets and battlements, which are purely for show, has been perfectly preserved as the typical English country house, partly because it has escaped military involvement but also ironically due to two centuries of neglect. During this period while the hall was unoccupied it stood frozen in time and escaped the eighteenth- and nineteenth-century fashionable architectural styles. So many of the young aristocracy of the day undertook the customary Grand European Tour as part of their education and this resulted in many properties in this country being demolished and rebuilt or radically altered.

A house on the site of Haddon Hall was recorded in the *Domesday Book*. At that time the manor was held by William Peverel, alleged illegitimate son of William the Conqueror. Little, if any, of this property remains today. Around 1153 Haddon was tenanted by William Avenel, who within 20 years had divided the manor between his sons-in-law, Richard Vernon and Simon Basset. The Basset line soon disappeared and the Vernon period at Haddon began. Little construction was undertaken at Haddon until 1370 when Richard Vernon commenced a period of building work which continued over the next few centuries as the Vernon family wealth increased with their investment in local lead mining. The Vernons also became major property owners in nearby towns such as Bakewell, and effectively they took control of the economic and political life of this part of Derbyshire. Indeed the autocratic nature of the last Vernon, Sir George, led to him becoming nicknamed 'King of the Peak'.

Unintentionally, Sir George sealed the transfer of the manor of Haddon from his family to the Manners, who remain in ownership today. Sir George, who was a Catholic, apparently took a dislike to one of the suitors of his youngest daughter and co-heiress, Dorothy. The gentleman in question was Sir John Manners, who was from a family of rich but Protestant landowners whose local power was the only rival to that of the Vernons. Although the truth has never come to light it is said in legend that at a party to celebrate the marriage of Sir George's eldest daughter, Dorothy and Sir John eloped

Haddon Hall

and married. Whatever the reality, in 1567 the hall did pass to Dorothy Manners (née Vernon) and this united the two most powerful local families.

In 1641 the grandson of Sir John, also Sir John, became the Earl of Rutland and he moved his household to Belvoir Castle in Lincolnshire. Later in 1703 a dukedom was conferred upon the family. It was the ninth duke in the 1920s who after two centuries of neglect turned his full energy into returning Haddon to its former glory and he also transferred the family back to Haddon.

ROUTE INSTRUCTIONS

1 From the car park return to Coombs Road and turn left onto Station Road and left again onto the A619. After crossing Bakewell Bridge turn left onto the riverside path. At a fork just before an open area bear left and follow the surfaced path around the back of the cricket pavilion and then round to the right away from the river and towards an adventure playground. At a T-junction in front of the playground turn left to enter a housing area. Cross over a road and take the path virtually opposite, which leads to Agricultural Way. Turn right onto the road and then left onto the A6.

2 In 75m at the end of the housing turn right by a public footpath sign for Over Haddon onto a rough track known as Intake Lane. Follow the bridleway as it climbs uphill for several kilometres to a lane. Turn left onto the lane and then right at a T-junction opposite Noton Barn Farm. The lane bends to the left and then to the right. On the right-hand bend climb a stile on the left and head across a field to a stile. Youlgreave and its church stand over to the left in the distance. In the next field walk half right to a stile by a public footpath sign. Walk across the middle of a field to reach a lane by the Lathkill Hotel and the houses of Over Haddon.

3 The route passes the front of the hotel and bears left at a fork. At the next two junctions bear left. At the second junction Lathkill Dale Craft Centre is on the right. Keep ahead at the next T-junction and then turn left by Yew Tree tea rooms. Follow the winding lane down to the River Lathkill. Turn left onto a surfaced path by a lodge and follow this delightful riverside path to a lane.

4 Turn right onto the lane and cross over Conksbury Bridge. When the lane bends to the

Bakewell Bridge

right, turn left onto a path with wire fencing on the left. Climb a stile and continue by a wall to a gate. A hundred metres after the gate turn left onto a track by a public footpath sign. Follow the bridleway across the River Wye and as it winds uphill through woodland to a metal gate at the top. There is a fork of bridleways after the gate. Bear to the right to walk along the right-hand edge of several fields. Haddon Hall gradually comes into view. Keep ahead at a crossroad of paths by a public footpath sign to a gate. Pass through the gate and continue downhill along a track to the A6.

5 Cross over this busy road with extreme care and turn left onto the pavement. The entrance to Haddon Hall is now on your right. Follow the A6 for 200m, and 75m before a right-hand bend road sign climb a stile in the wall by a public footpath sign to Sheepbridge on the right. Follow the path down across the River Wye and to a lane. Turn right onto the lane and then turn left in 20m at a public footpath sign for Coombs Road. Keep to the yellow waymarker posts with the winding river on your left over a footbridge. When Bakewell church spire comes into view head across the meadow to a hedge and walk with the hedge on your right to join the surfaced Agricultural Way in a parking area. Continue to the Agricultural and Business Centre, which can be seen ahead, and turn left over a footbridge opposite the centre to return to the long-stay car park.

Refreshments:	Pubs and cafes in Bakewell, and a tea room, Lathkill Hotel and Lathkill Dale Craft Centre at Over Haddon
Toilets:	Car park at Over Haddon
Key Features:	Sections of the River Wye and River Lathkill; Bakewell; Lathkill Dale Craft Centre (01629 812390); Haddon Hall (01629 812855)

WALK 17
Wingfield Manor and Crich

Distance:	12km/7½ miles
Start:	Roadside parking in Crich village centre near the Baptist Chapel
Map:	OS Explorer 269 Chesterfield & Alfreton
Terrain:	A moderately undulating walk mainly across fields with a potentially very muddy section as you skirt around Wingfield Manor

Crich is a large hilltop village and former market town overlooking the Derwent Valley. Its main claims to fame are that it is the home of the National Tramway Museum and that it is the setting for 'Cardale' in the TV *Peak Practice* medical drama. The museum occupies the floor of George Stephenson's Crich Cliff Quarry, which served Stephenson's limekilns along the Cromford Canal in the valley bottom via a steep railway.

George Stephenson and his equally gifted son Robert have gone down in British history as two of the most outstanding civil engineers this country has ever produced. George is popularly acclaimed as the 'Father of the Railways' for his pioneering and significant contribution to the age of railway mania. He was responsible for the world's first public steam locomotive, *Locomotion*, and later his world famous *Rocket*. Later in Stephenson's life the northeastern corner of Derbyshire was to benefit from his railway engineering feats, and the local economy benefited from his exploitation of various natural resources.

The ruins of Wingfield Manor, a large medieval country mansion, stand magnificently on a hilltop overlooking the village of South Wingfield. Today the manor incorporates a working farm and has been open to the public since 1995 in the hands of English Heritage. Wingfield Manor cannot be accessed directly from this walk unless you leave the route on reaching the B5035 and turn left for several hundred metres and then left again up a driveway, which is signposted for Wingfield Manor. Please only visit the manor during official opening hours and respect the privacy of the owners and keep to visitor routes. In recent years the manor has been used as a location for *Peak Practice* and for Zeffirelli's *Jane Eyre*. What remains of the

Wingfield Manor

manor house is well worth a visit, especially to see the large Great Hall with its vaulted undercroft and the High Tower with its exceptional views, which are fine testaments to Wingfield Manor in its heyday.

The manor stands on the site of a Norman castle and was built in the mid-fifteenth century by Ralph, Lord Cromwell, Treasurer of England to Henry VI, who was one of the most powerful men in England of his time. His family home was actually Tattershall Castle in Lincolnshire, but he acquired the manor of South Wingfield in 1429 to satisfy his hunting pastime and to create a convenient hunting lodge for the Royal Forest of Duffield Frith. The hunting lodge soon became an imposing palace for Cromwell to hold court.

On Cromwell's death in 1456, as he had no heirs, the manor was sold to the Earl of Shrewsbury. The Sixth Earl of Shrewsbury, who was head of one of the oldest and richest families in England, was to become the fourth husband of Bess of Hardwick from Hardwick Hall. Shortly after his marriage to Bess, Elizabeth I saddled the earl with the task of acting as custodian to Mary Stuart (Mary Queen of Scots). As her gaoler the earl moved Mary around his various properties and she was imprisoned at Wingfield in 1569, 1584 and 1585. It was during this final stay at Wingfield that Anthony Babington, an attendant of the Shrewsburys, developed an infatuation with

Mary and allegedly visited her on a number of occasions dressed as a gypsy. These visits are of historical importance as Anthony Babington was to become ringleader of the famous Babington Plot to assassinate Elizabeth I.

During the Civil War, both the royalists and parliamentarians held Wingfield Manor at various times; therefore, having been built by a Cromwell, the manor was the victim of another Cromwell, or at least his Roundhead troops. After the restoration of the monarchy in 1660 Wingfield Manor was sold to the Halton family, although it was unoccupied from the 1770s and later became a farm when the Haltons sold it.

ROUTE INSTRUCTIONS

1 Walk up Sandy Lane next to the Baptist Chapel. Turn left at the second public footpath sign on the left, which is signposted for Chadwick Nick. Pass through a squeeze stile and follow the left-hand edge of a number of fields across the Tors with extensive views in both directions to reach a lane. Turn right onto Chadwick Nick Lane and when the lane bends to the right, turn left by a public footpath sign.

2 Follow the left-hand edge of two fields to climb a stile. Turn left after the stile and soon enter woodland. You briefly emerge from the woodland into a more open area before quickly passing through trees once again. At a fork bear to the right and then maintain direction at a crossroad of paths. Drop down a grassy hillside and at a fork in 100m bear to the right back into woodland. At a junction of paths turn left and then at the fork immediately in front of you bear to the right. The path drops down to a stile, which you climb and follow the path to the right to a gate. Turn right and cross a bridge over the Cromford Canal. To join the canal towpath turn right and then turn right again to pass under the bridge you have just walked over.

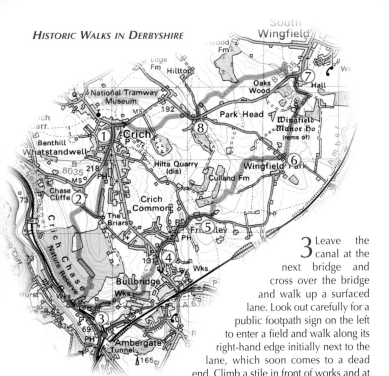

3 Leave the canal at the next bridge and cross over the bridge and walk up a surfaced lane. Look out carefully for a public footpath sign on the left to enter a field and walk along its right-hand edge initially next to the lane, which soon comes to a dead end. Climb a stile in front of works and at a T-junction in 10m turn left in front of a wire fence. Soon climb another stile into a field and follow an uphill grassy path as it bends to the right. By the bend there are two paths. Take the higher path, which leads to a track on a ridge in 75m. Turn right onto the track and 40m after the track bends to the left climb a stile next to a large metal gate on the right. Turn left and later pass through a squeeze stile at the side of a wooden gate to join a track which is walled on the right and fenced on the left and maintain direction to reach a road near Fritchley.

4 Cross over the lane onto Allen Lane, but as this is a blind bend it would be wise to move away from the bend before crossing and walk through

Fritchley passing the Red Lion pub on the left. After passing through the village, which was an important centre for the Quaker movement in the nineteenth and early twentieth centuries, disregard the T-junction for Crich and pass a farm before reaching a public footpath which crosses the lane.

5 Turn left onto a track and pass through a gap at the side of a gate into a field. Follow the left-hand edge of the field and climb a stile. Turn right and walk along the right-hand side of a field to a track. Turn right onto a walled track with distant views of Wingfield Manor. In 75m turn left through a gate and follow a grassy path to the far right-hand corner of the field. Pass through a gate and at a wall corner turn left to walk along the left-hand edge of a field. Pass through a squeeze stile at the side of a gate and follow a track first to the right and then to the left as it crosses a stream. After the stream bear half right to a stile in 40m. Climb this stile and a further stile in 15m and then maintain direction to a lane.

6 Turn right onto the lane by Mill Cottage and then turn left by a public footpath sign in 10m to follow the left-hand edge of two fields and the right-hand edge of a third field. After the next field you will reach Wingfield Manor and will probably have a mud bath created by cattle to negotiate as you pass to the left of the manor to a junction of paths by a signpost. Take the left-hand fork of bridleways, dropping gently downhill to climb a stile by the side of a gate. Turn left onto a track passing Wingfield Hall on the right before reaching the B5035. If you turn around at this point there are fine views of the manor perched up on the hilltop. Dismantled parts of the manor have been incorporated into the hall.

7 Cross over the road and turn left for 100m to reach a public footpath sign for Inns Lane on

the right. Follow the left-hand edge of a field to a stile. Climb the stile and head half left over to a footbridge in 40m. At the fork immediately after the footbridge bear to the right and follow the left-hand edge of three fields, the right-hand edge of the next field and then walk across the middle of two fields to a T-junction of paths. Turn right and then pass through a gap in the hedge on the left in 50m. Climb a stile into the next field and before the field corner pass through a squeeze stile on the left. Walk along the right-hand edge of a field and join a track as you pass to the right of Rough Farm. Thirty metres after the farm pass through a squeeze stile and turn left onto a track.

8 Turn right onto the road at Park Head and then turn left at a public footpath sign for Crich. Walk along the right-hand edge of a number fields before passing through a squeeze stile and following the left-hand edge of a field. Just before reaching a stream bear left through a gate and then bear half right to cross over the stream. In 20m cross over a track at a signpost for Crich Cross. Ten metres after the track look out carefully for a yellow waymarker on the right and follow it into a field. Initially keep to the left-hand edge of the field, but shortly after passing a marker post the path swings to the right to the B5035. Turn left onto the road and then turn left again at Crich Cross by the Jovial Dutchman pub to return to the starting point.

Refreshments:	Public houses, shop and tea rooms at Crich and public house at Frichley
Toilets:	Crich village between the Jovial Dutchman and the Black Swan
Key Features:	The village of Crich and the nearby National Tramway Museum (01773 852565) and Wingfield Manor (01773 832060)

WALK 18
Longshaw Estate and Padley Chapel

Distance:	12km/7½ miles or 7km/4½ miles
Start:	The Longshaw Estate car park off the B6055
Map:	OS Explorer OL24 The Peak District White Peak Area
Terrain:	There are two moderate climbs and several steep downhill sections on this varied walk. In route instruction 2 there is a short boggy section.

The National Trust has maintained the 1600 acre Longshaw Estate since the early 1970s. It was once part of a much larger estate owned by the Dukes of Rutland, which was sold and broken up in 1927. Longshaw Lodge, built in 1827 as a shooting lodge, is the focal point for the estate with the National Trust Visitor Centre next to it. Today it has been converted into private flats. The area around the visitor centre is ablaze with rhododendrons in May/June. Every September on the meadow below the lodge the country's longest established sheepdog trials are held, which first took place in 1898.

Padley Chapel, formerly a gatehouse, is the only remaining part of a fourteenth-century manor house and home of the Fitzherbert family. During the reign of Queen Elizabeth I, Sir Thomas Fitzherbert owned Padley Hall. In 1588, the year of the Spanish Armada, when Catholic persecution in England was rife, Sir Thomas, a devout Roman Catholic, was found to be providing shelter to two priests, Robert Ludlam and Richard Garlick. The priests were arrested and taken to Derby where they were tried, hung, drawn and quartered. Sir Thomas was

In this area large numbers of abandoned grindstones can be found from the days when gritstone quarrying flourished for building materials, grindstones and millstones. The need for grindstones declined after the introduction of rolling mills in the mid-nineteenth century. The grindstones that have been left scattered across the countryside, which were probably imperfect rejects, now act as an ornamental feature to the landscape as well as a reminder of the area's industrial past.

Padley Chapel

imprisoned and died in the Tower of London in 1591.

The hall later fell into ruin and at one time it was even used as a cowshed, but in 1933 the Roman Catholic Diocese of Nottingham purchased the simple barn-like structure of the gatehouse and restored it as a chapel and shrine to the two Padley martyrs. Each year the terrible persecution of these two priests is commemorated at an annual pilgrimage at Padley Chapel on the Thursday nearest 12 July.

The view at Bolehill of the Derwent and Hope valleys is aptly named 'Surprise View'. There were once extensive quarries at Bolehill, which was the centre of local millstone manufacturing for many years. Today more than 200 millstones litter the track from Surprise View to Bolehill. The Bolehill quarry area is a favourite haunt of rock climbers.

ROUTE INSTRUCTIONS

1 Follow the path from the back of the car park, which is signposted for the visitor centre. At a T-junction turn right if you wish to view the visitor

centre at this point, otherwise turn left into woodland. At the end of the trees pass through a gate and continue ahead across an open area. At a fork of paths bear left to reach the B6055. Head across two junctions to a large white gate and National Trust sign for White Edge Moor. Walk along a track towards White Edge Lodge. Ignore the fork to the left just before the lodge and pass the lodge. The rough track then becomes a grassy track. Keep ahead at a T-junction to reach the B6054.

2 Cross over the road and turn left and then right in 10m through a gate back onto the Longshaw Estate to follow a broad track. When the track disappears into woodland there is a stile on the left. Climb the stile and follow a path moving slightly away from a wall on the right, which at first is paved and can become a little boggy, down towards some trees at the head of a valley. Bear to the right, at first without the aid of a visible path, down into the valley, which soon starts to drop down steeply and

involves a little bit of scrambling over rocks with a stream on your left. At the bottom of the hill you reach the B6521.

109

3 Turn left and then right in 10m to join a steep downhill surfaced path which leads down to Grindleford Station. Turn right at the T-junction to pass the cafe on your right and cross over the railway line. When the surfaced lane ends continue along a rough track over a stream and past Padley Mill. At a T-junction of tracks turn right if you wish to complete the shorter version of this walk. Otherwise continue along this track to pass Padley Chapel and Greenwood Farm, which is in the ownership of the National Trust, for several kilometres to reach the A625. Along this track there are a few examples of abandoned millstones.

4 Turn right onto the road to walk uphill on the pavement with Millstone Edge in front of you. Ignore the first stile on the right and continue to the next stile 100m further on by a National Trust sign for Bolehill, which is just before a sign indicating a sharp left-hand bend. Follow a grassy track, disregarding any offshoots, to eventually drop down to a T-junction. Turn right along a path that winds through trees with a ruined building on the right. When a faint path comes in on the left in 75m bear left to drop steeply downhill to a

Abandoned millstones

T-junction in front of a building. Turn right and then bear left at a fork to walk with a wall on the left to reach a track by a cattle grid.

5 Turn left onto the track and retrace your steps back past Padley Chapel to the T-junction of tracks mentioned in instruction 3 for the shorter walk. Turn left at this T-junction and head uphill. When the track ends pass through a gate into Padley Gorge. This ancient woodland is a Site of Special Scientific Interest and is one of the most important sites in Derbyshire for the ornithologist and botanist. Continue climbing up into woodland and maintain direction along the main path through the gorge, later walking close to Burbage Brook. Pass through a gate at the end of the woodland into a delightful open area, which is popular with families for sunbathing and children playing in the brook. After 200m cross a footbridge over the brook and head uphill to a gate onto a road.

6 Turn right onto the road and then left in 10m through a gate. Follow the path to pass through another gate and skirt around the edge of a lake before it bends to the left towards Longshaw Lodge. Pass through another gate and when you are faced with a choice of three gates negotiate the gate to the left, which leads to the National Trust Visitor Centre. Turn left in front of the visitor centre and then right in a few metres at a T-junction. Then in 20m turn left at a T-junction to return to the car park.

Refreshments:	National Trust Visitor Centre near the starting point or Grindleford Station cafe
Toilets:	National Trust Visitor Centre near the starting point or Grindleford Station cafe
Key Features:	The Longshaw Estate and National Trust Visitor Centre (01433 631708); Padley Gorge; Padley Chapel

WALK 19
Hardwick Hall

Distance:	14km/9 miles
Start:	Hardwick Country Park – Hardwick Ponds
Map:	OS Explorer 269 Chesterfield & Alfreton
Terrain:	A long but easy-going walk on trails, across fields and through the Hardwick Estate

Hardwick Hall survives today with many of its original contents as listed in an inventory taken in 1601. It has a unique antiquarian atmosphere and escaped modernisation, without being neglected, during its ownership by the Cavendish family (the current Dukes of Devonshire) which ended in 1959, when the hall was accepted in lieu of death duties and handed over to the National Trust.

In the late sixteenth century, following the dissolution of the monasteries, a new Elizabethan landed class began to emerge who built large grand mansions on their landscaped country estates. This was a time when there was a clear and competitive link between building and status. Building was on a scale for show rather than function, and a lofty position could elevate and advertise wealth and social position. The ultimate aim was to attract a royal visit with all its attendant opportunities and favours. Bess of Hardwick and Hardwick Hall provide us with a perfect example of this social structure. Indeed, probably no house in the country is so indelibly linked with one person, and to find two large houses so close together produces a truly impressive effect.

Bess, daughter of a Derbyshire squire, owned a small manor house on the site of the Old Hall. She married four times, each time to a husband more wealthy and influential than the last, and she outlived them all to become the richest and most powerful woman in England after Queen Elizabeth I. Bess was a formidable business woman, a builder of great houses, a collector, and was highly ambitious both for herself on the marriage market and for her children. Her genetic engineering had important dynastic consequences as Bess and her second husband, William Cavendish, were the founders of the

Hardwick Hall

ducal families of Devonshire, Newcastle and Portland. She was sent to the Tower of London twice by the Queen for attempts to advance her wealth and prosperity.

Standing on top of a windblown scarp, Hardwick Hall, 'more glass than wall', is one of the finest and most complete examples of Elizabethan architecture, with an emphasis on symmetry that history and chance have miraculously preserved. Its majestic qualities led to it being regarded by contemporaries as a masterpiece of innovative features and ingenious design. It has six imposing towers and the huge initials ES crowning the roofline. Unusually for the time the building was a storey higher than the norm and contained a vast area of windows and glass. Glass was an expensive material of the day and to use it on such a scale was another display of extravagance.

D H Lawrence (1885–1930), who was born and lived 12 miles/20km from Teversal, set his last and most controversial novel, *Lady Chatterley's Lover,* in the rural Nottinghamshire coalfields. The book was published privately in 1928 but it was not for over 30 years that the complete version was published following an infamous trial, which unsuccessfully attempted to ban it on the grounds of obscenity. Many of the important locations in the book can be identified locally, for example Teversal was referred to as Tevershall; Teversal Manor was

Wragby Hall, home of Sir Clifford and Lady Chatterley; the cottage of Oliver Mellors (the gamekeeper) was set at Norwood; Norwood was where Mellors had his hut of rustic poles; and Hardwick Hall was Chadwick Hall.

ROUTE INSTRUCTIONS

1 Start from the information point/toilet block and take the path to the left around Miller Pond. Follow the path around the pond and shortly after passing through a second kissing gate turn left at a crossroad of paths. When you see a gate and kissing gate in front of you, look to the left for another kissing gate and go through it. Follow the gentle uphill path to another kissing gate in the top left-hand corner of the field. Go through this gate and cross over the road and continue ahead between trees. For the first 100m a path cannot be seen on the ground, but if you keep roughly halfway between the road on the right and the fence on the left a small marker post comes into

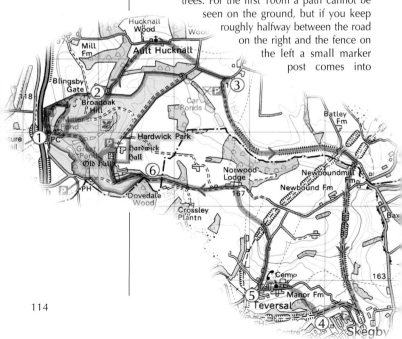

view. A path then becomes visible and as you continue to climb it begins to swing to the left to a kissing gate in front of a cottage.

2 Follow the well-surfaced track to a lane. Ault Hucknall church can be seen on the lane. Turn right onto the lane and after 200m turn right through a gate. Take the right-hand fork across a field to a stile. Climb the stile and cross a second field to another stile. After crossing the stile turn right onto a lane. Ignore the right fork, which leads to Hardwick Hall, and follow the road round to the left, signposted Rowthorne, for several hundred metres.

3 Turn right into the Rowthorne Trail car park and after 50m take the track to the left signposted 'The Trail'. Follow the trail across a number of stiles for 4km/2½ miles until you reach the other end of the trail by a signpost. Bear to the left to a stile and drop down onto a lane in 20m. Turn right onto the lane, and 200m after a railway bridge turn right onto the Teversal Trail for several kilometres to a large triangular junction of paths. Here turn right and then in 20m pass through a gate on the right, which is signposted for the Teversal Visitor Centre.

4 When a public footpath crosses the trail turn right and walk down some steps to a stile. Climb the stile and follow the path over a footbridge. Turn left after the footbridge and follow the field edge around to the right with Coppy Wood on the left. On reaching a corner of the wood the path heads across the middle of the field to a stile. Climb the stile and at the road junction in front of you take the first left into Teversal, passing Manor Farm in 50m on the left and St Katherine's Church on the right. Pass through a gate and at a T-junction of surfaced paths keep ahead to reach a road. Maintain direction on the pavement to a T-junction and turn right as signposted for Pleasley.

5 The headstocks of Pleasley can be seen half right. The lane drops downhill and then climbs back uphill. Forty metres after passing a white house climb a stile by a public footpath sign on the left onto a track. Cross a bridge over the Teversal Trail and when the hedge on both sides ends turn left along a field edge. Just before a hedge corner turn right to walk across the middle of a field towards Norwood Lodge with Norwood behind it. Turn left onto a surfaced lane by the lodge. After the last house the lane becomes a rough track. Follow it to a gate and turn right over a stile.

6 The path passes through Lady Spencer's Wood to a stile. Climb the stile and follow the path ahead across a field to a kissing gate and onto a driveway of the Hardwick Estate. Turn right and walk uphill crossing a cattle grid to soon reach the Old Hall on the left and Hardwick Hall on the right. Almost opposite the entrance to Hardwick Hall a downhill path can be seen 50m to the left. Follow the path through a kissing gate and continue downhill to another kissing gate in the fence on your right just after the first Row Pond. Take the path between the first and second Row Pond and turn left to follow the edge of the pond. (Ignore the clearer track ahead.) Follow the edge of another pond and then continue to the Great Pond. Go through a kissing gate and cross a footbridge before arriving back at the car park. Before leaving the Great Pond turn around for a magnificent view of both the Old Hall and Hardwick Hall.

Refreshments:	None
Toilets:	Hardwick Ponds car park
Key Features:	Hardwick Hall (01246 850430); Hardwick Old Hall (01246 850431); Hardwick Ponds; Ault Hucknall Church; Teversal

Walk 20
Bolsover Castle

Distance:	7km/4½ miles
Start:	Stockley Trail car park just off the A632 on Riverside Way between Bolsover and the M1
Map:	OS Explorer 269 Chesterfield & Alfreton
Terrain:	Easy trail walking followed by a climb up to Palterton and then field and road walking

Despite its commanding position Bolsover Castle is very much a castle in name only as the remains are that of a mock medieval country house celebrating romance and chivalry, built on the site of a twelfth-century castle. It is elaborately decorated in the Jacobean style, although no furniture remains as this was all moved to Welbeck Abbey, which became the owner's main home during the eighteenth century. The sense of theatre created by this fantasy seventeenth-century property contrasts strongly with the surrounding legacy of the industrial past of more recent centuries. From 1755 to 1945 the castle was in the hands of the Portland family, who transferred it to the nation. The castle is now looked after by English Heritage and it is without doubt a truly unique property. English Heritage has recently completed a £3 million renovation and has built a new visitor centre.

The mood of the castle has been encapsulated by many. In his masque *Loves Welcome To Bolsover*, written for the visit of Charles I, Ben Jonson reminds us 'This is not a warlike place, much of its imagery is intellectual, sensual and designed to evoke the virtues of romantic love'. Sacheverell Sitwell from nearby Renishaw commented that Bolsover had 'a ghostly poetry that fires the imagination, that can never be forgotten and that never cools'.

Bolsover Castle, one of England's finest late Renaissance monuments, is an astonishing complex of sandstone buildings that stands dramatically on the top of a magnesian limestone ridge in the small market town of Bolsover, dominating the landscape for miles around. Effectively two contrasting and fascinating houses were built, one a dream romantic folly with lavish interior decoration and the other a huge palatial terrace range for entertaining and accommodating important guests.

Bolsover Castle

The town of Bolsover was first granted a market charter in 1225. During the eighteenth century it was famous for its buckles and spurs and the manufacture of clay pipes. From the late nineteenth century the town grew rapidly with the expanding coal mining industry. Indeed the model village of New Bolsover built by the Bolsover Colliery Company is one of the finest and most important examples of colliery architecture in this country. It is of such great historical and architectural value that the entire village is listed.

The Stockley Trail follows the former Glapwell Colliery branch line and was acquired by Derbyshire County Council from British Rail in 1993.

Sutton Scarsdale Hall was once one of the most magnificent properties in Derbyshire and is now in the hands of English Heritage. Nicholas Leake, who was the fourth and last Earl of Scarsdale, built the hall in 1774. In 1824 the hall passed to descendants of the famous industrialist Richard Arkwright and it remained in his family until 1926. A speculator, who sold everything that could be removed, then purchased it. The ruins were saved by Sir Osbert Sitwell from Renishaw Hall after the Second World War on the day before they were due to be pulled down. Sir Reresby Sitwell then passed the shell to the Ministry of the Environment.

ROUTE INSTRUCTIONS

1 From the car park follow the trail away from the A632. At a fork bear to the right for 100m to a viewpoint and an excellent set of information boards. Retrace your steps to the junction and turn right to reach a rough track. The Stockley Trail continues on the opposite side of the track, but a diversion to Carr Vale Nature Reserve can be made at this point by taking the path to the right, which leads to the reserve in 100m. At a crossroad of paths another short diversion can be made to the right to visit the new Flashes; otherwise continue ahead and cross over Carr Lane. Sutton Scarsdale Hall can be seen over to the right beyond the M1.

2 Ignore the first path, which now crosses the trail, but turn left at the next crossroads as signposted to Palterton. Follow the left-hand edge of a field which bends first to the right, and then when it bends to the left by a marker post keep ahead to

Sutton Scarsdale Hall

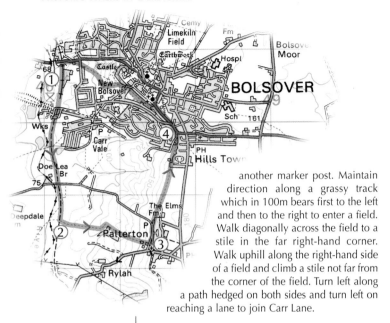

another marker post. Maintain direction along a grassy track which in 100m bears first to the left and then to the right to enter a field. Walk diagonally across the field to a stile in the far right-hand corner. Walk uphill along the right-hand side of a field and climb a stile not far from the corner of the field. Turn left along a path hedged on both sides and turn left on reaching a lane to join Carr Lane.

3 Turn left onto Carr Lane and ignore the road to the right called Pennine View. A few metres further on bear to the right at a fork onto a No Through Road. The lane soon ends and you pass through a kissing gate into a field. Pass farm buildings on your right and make for a large metal gate in the far right-hand corner. Climb the stile and follow the clearly defined track into a housing area. Maintain direction until you reach Langwith Road.

4 Turn left and when the road bends to the right bear to the left onto High Street by the brown tourist sign for Bolsover Castle. When the road bends to the right, if you wish to visit Bolsover Castle or its visitor centre follow the road for 30m and the entrance is on the left, otherwise bear to

Bolsover Castle

the left onto Castle Lane. The road bends to the right and then to the left. On the left-hand bend turn right onto a surfaced path. When the surfaced path ends walk downhill along the left-hand edge of a field with magnificent views of Bolsover Castle behind you. Turn right by a marker post and then at the next marker post close to a seat turn left and walk across a field towards a hedge corner and then keep the hedge on your left to reach a road. Turn right and then in 10m turn left at a public footpath sign to walk through a field along a surfaced path to the A632. Cross over the road and turn left along the pavement and walk to the roundabout. Turn left and return to the car park either by walking along Riverside Way or by joining the Stockley Trail.

Refreshments:	Pubs at Bolsover and a cafe at Bolsover Castle Visitor Centre
Toilets:	Bolsover Castle Visitor Centre
Key Features:	Bolsover Castle (01246 822844) and a section of the Stockley Trail

Distance:	11.5km/7 miles
Start:	Tissington Trail car park, Tissington, or Alsop Station car park on the A515
Map:	OS Explorer OL24 The Peak District White Peak Area
Terrain:	Pleasant field and trail walking

Tissington is without doubt one of the most beautiful villages in England, almost too perfect to be true, except that it does not have a pub! This is Fitzherbert country as the family have occupied Tissington Hall for five centuries. Built in 1609 and extended several times over the centuries, the hall is an elegant Jacobean manor house which replaced a moated manor house to the north of the church. The hall acts as the focal point for the village and the current owner, Sir Richard Fitzherbert, has in recent years allowed the public to view some of the rooms at certain times of the year.

The Fitzherberts came over to England with William the Conqueror and settled in Derbyshire. George III conferred the baronetcy on William Fitzherbert in 1784. Successive baronets have tended diligently to the building and maintenance of the neat stone cottages, which are scattered haphazardly to produce an idyllic well-managed estate village, complete with village green, duck pond, church and plenty of trees and greenery. The Norman tower of the Parish Church of St Mary, which was heavily restored in the mid-nineteenth century, contains many monuments to the Fitzherbert family. The size of the estate has reduced from its peak in 1850 of about 4000 acres, largely due to sales enforced by twentieth-century death duties, to 2400 acres today, comprising 13 farms and 40 cottages.

The village is especially popular at Ascensiontide as the ancient Derbyshire tradition of well dressing still continues at Tissington, when five wells are dressed elaborately with thousands of flower petals. Indeed Tissington is the first recorded place in the Peak District where this ceremony took place.

The Tissington Trail is a 21km/13 mile scenic route across the rolling countryside of the White Peak, which follows the line of the former Ashbourne to Buxton railway line. This was one of the last railway lines to be built during the Railway Age by the London and North

Western Railway Company, which opened in 1899. The railway was never more than a branch line carrying milk to large towns and limestone from local quarries to the kilns and crushing plants at Buxton. The line was closed in 1963 and was then reopened by the Peak National Park as a leisure route in 1971. The traffic-free route runs alongside Dovedale from Ashbourne and climbs to join the High Peak Trail at Parsley Hay for the last mile of the route. The trail, which takes its name from the village of Tissington, sweeps around the outskirts of the village.

ROUTE INSTRUCTIONS

1 Turn left out of the car park onto the road and pass the village pond on the left. At the end of the pond turn right, passing first the tea room on the left and then Tissington Hall. At a T-junction turn right and then bear to the left at a fork onto a No Through Road. The surfaced lane later becomes a rough track and crosses a bridge over the Tissington Trail. Climb a stile at the side of a cattle grid and follow the track as it bends to the

Tissington Hall (front)

123

left. On the bend turn right at a signpost for Parwich and walk downhill to a stile at the side of a gate, passing Shaw's Farm on the left. Follow the right-hand side of a field and pass through a squeeze stile. Head for a footbridge over Bletch Brook. The route then begins to climb uphill, passing a telegraph pole, and reaches a stile at the top of the hill to the right of two large trees.

2 Walk along the left-hand side of two fields and then maintain direction, dropping downhill with views of the pretty limestone village of Parwich and the Church of St Peter to a footpath sign next to a squeeze stile. The church is of Norman origins but was largely rebuilt in 1873. Continue to a lane and turn right and then left in 20m. Turn left at a T-junction and climb a stile on the right in a few metres. Follow a grassy path to a gate and keep straight ahead across two small fields to another gate. At the other side of the next field pass through a squeeze stile onto a track which

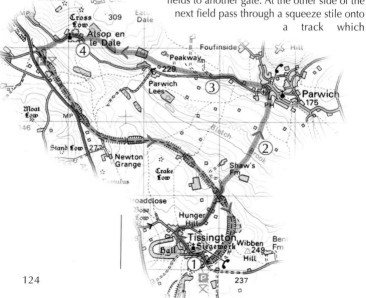

leads to a lane. Turn right onto the lane. Ignore the first public footpath sign on the right at the brow of the hill and continue on to the next, which is signposted for Alsop en le Dale in 200m.

Tissington Hall (rear)

3 Pass through a gate onto a track, but do not follow the track. Instead bear left and walk parallel to the lane to a stile. Keep ahead to cross over a track and pass through a squeeze stile. Continue on, crossing a footbridge, and follow a faint grassy track half right to cross over yet another track. Pass Peakway on the right to reach another squeeze stile. Cross the middle of the next field and negotiate another squeeze stile to follow a path to the right of a hill through a young plantation. After the plantation maintain direction across a field to a public footpath sign and follow the left-hand edge of a field, passing a clump of trees. The route then

heads across scrubland before emerging into a field. Follow the left-hand edge of this field to a stile in a wall by a public footpath sign halfway along the field. In the next field head half right to a stile and then in the next walk half left to a stile. Climb the stile onto a lane in Alsop en le Dale.

4 Turn right onto the lane and pass the Norman church of St Michael on the left, which was substantially rebuilt in Victorian times. Opposite the church is Alsop Hall which is now a private residence. At a public footpath sign on a right-hand bend turn left. Follow the right-hand edge of a field heading uphill towards a clump of trees. Pass through a gap in the far right-hand corner of the field and continue uphill, soon reaching the Tissington Trail. Turn left onto the trail close to Alsop Station car park (alternative starting point) and follow it for 5km/3 miles back to the starting point.

Refreshments:	Tissington Trail car park, a tea room at Tissington and a pub at Parwich
Toilets:	Tissington Trail car park
Key Features:	The village of Tissington and its hall (01325 352200 for opening times – specified days during June to August) and a section of the Tissington Trail

WALK 22
Eyam

Distance:	10.5km/6½ miles
Start:	Car park on Hawkhill Road, Eyam, opposite Eyam Museum
Map:	OS Explorer OL24 The Peak District White Peak Area
Terrain:	A steep climb up onto Eyam Moor at the beginning of the walk and an even steeper descent back into the village at the end. In between the two hills is excellent easy moorland walking.

Eyam, pronounced 'Eem', is famed as the Plague Village. Other towns and villages across the country suffered worse epidemics during the Great Plague, but the dramatic tales of the heroic self-sacrifice alongside desperation and loss of the inhabitants of Eyam has put the village into the history books and high on the agenda of visitors. Current medical thinking casts doubt on whether it actually was the plague which devastated the village; nonetheless it was a touching and tragic event of which there are many poignant reminders today.

According to tradition the plague was imported into Eyam in 1665 by fleas festering in a box of cloth sent from the capital to George Viccars, the local tailor. As the cloth was damp Viccars hung it up in front of his fire to dry. Several days later the tailor was the first victim to lose his life. The plague quickly took hold of the village and the panic of the villagers is easy to imagine. It was only the intervention of two clergymen that ensured the survival of the village and, by containing the plague, prevented its spread to other communities.

The newly appointed rector, the Rev William Mompesson, obtained the co-operation of his Nonconformist predecessor, Thomas Stanley. This meant burying their deep doctrinal differences to persuade the villagers to take the courageous decision not to flee the village and to impose a voluntary quarantine upon themselves to allow the plague to run its course. They also agreed to bury their own dead and change the pattern of their worship to contain the spread of the infection. This brave action saw the death of 259 people between September 1665 and October 1666, perhaps a third of the population, but the disease was successfully kept

Eyam's plague cottages

within the boundaries of the village. Seventy-six families were affected and some were completely wiped out – Elizabeth Hancock buried her husband and six children in eight days. These graves are now known as the Riley Graves and are situated about a kilometre from the village centre. An annual plague commemoration service is held in late August to coincide with the well dressing at Cucklett Delph, a limestone crag near the village where services were held in the open air during the plague. During the isolation food and other supplies were left at strategic points on the parish boundary, one of them known as Mompesson's Well, which is high above the village.

Eyam was once busy with local lead mining, quarrying, silk weaving and shoemaking. Sitting at the foot of Eyam Moor the village is strung out along one long main street lined by attractive and well-preserved seventeenth- and eighteenth-century gritstone cottages. Some of the houses have plaques on the wall outside giving details of their involvement in the plague – the cottage where the first victim lived is called Plague Cottage. The Miner's Arms pub built in 1630 is supposed to be one of Derbyshire's most haunted buildings.

The Church of St Lawrence contains Saxon and Norman fonts but it is mainly thirteenth and fourteenth century. Thomas Stanley, though not a plague victim himself, is buried in the churchyard amongst many of those who died in the plague, including Mompesson's wife. Also in the churchyard there is a magnificent and intricately carved seventh-century Saxon cross and a beautiful sundial on the wall of the church. Inside the church is a book containing the names of all the people who died in the plague, Mompesson's chair and an exhibition on the plague. The small Eyam Museum tells the full story of the village from prehistoric times to the Industrial Revolution. Eyam Hall was built shortly after

Saxon cross, Eyam churchyard

129

the plague in 1675 and has always been the home of the Wright family. The current owners inherited the hall in 1990 and opened it to the public in 1992 for guided tours. The old stables of the manor house have been converted into a craft centre.

ROUTE INSTRUCTIONS

1 Turn right out of the car park onto Hawkhill Road and head uphill. When the road bends to the right keep ahead on a No Through Road. When the surfaced lane ends continue climbing along a track which bends to the right and then to the left before reaching Highcliffe Farm. Turn right onto the lane and look out carefully for a stile on the left in several hundred metres. Climb the stile and walk along the right-hand edge of a field with a mast over to the left to reach a track known as Sir William Hill Road. It has never been established which Sir William this road was named after as there are several local candidates.

2 Climb the stile on the opposite side of the track to enter Eyam Moor. A clear path heads across level ground over the moor to reach a superb vantage point of the Derwent Valley. This moor has many Bronze Age remains including a stone circle. From here continue ahead, dropping downhill to a junction of paths and a metal gate 30m further on. Climb a stile at the side of the gate and follow a path along the edge of a ridge by a wall which bends to the right by a stile at the side of a gate. The path then begins to drop downhill and later bends to the left to descend through bracken into the valley bottom. Near the valley bottom the path swings to the right to a T-junction. Turn right here to reach Stoke Ford in a few metres.

3 Do not cross over the bridge but bear to the right to walk initially with the brook on your

left uphill along the side of the valley on a distinct path to reach a stile. Climb the

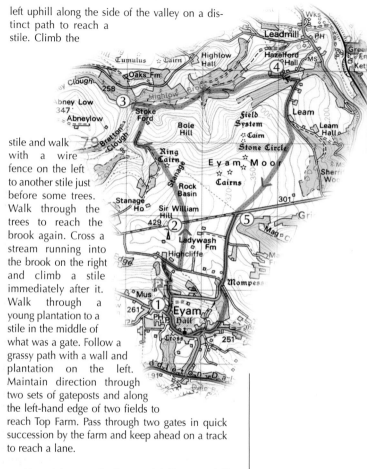

stile and walk with a wire fence on the left to another stile just before some trees. Walk through the trees to reach the brook again. Cross a stream running into the brook on the right and climb a stile immediately after it. Walk through a young plantation to a stile in the middle of what was a gate. Follow a grassy path with a wall and plantation on the left. Maintain direction through two sets of gateposts and along the left-hand edge of two fields to reach Top Farm. Pass through two gates in quick succession by the farm and keep ahead on a track to reach a lane.

4 Turn right onto the lane and follow it uphill and around a sharp bend. The lane passes Leam Farm, and then opposite the next farm buildings there is a stile on the right by a signpost for Sir William Hill Road. Climb the stile and turn left to

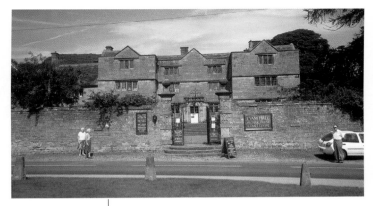

Eyam Hall

follow an obvious path back across Eyam Moor, later walking with a wire fence on the left to reach a road on a bend with the track called Sir William Hill Road on the right.

5 Ignore the track and continue ahead along Edge Road to eventually reach Mompesson's Well on the right 100m before a T-junction. Keep ahead at the T-junction but 40m further on turn left by a public footpath sign into woodland with Hollow Brook on the right to begin the descent back to Eyam. At a fork keep right and when the village of Eyam comes into view keep ahead at a T-junction to reach Riley Back Lane. Turn right at a T-junction and right again at the next junction to walk along Church Street, passing the church, the Plague Cottages and Eyam Hall before turning right back onto Hawkhill Road.

Refreshments:	Pubs and cafes in Eyam
Toilets:	Car park on Hawkhill Road, Eyam
Key Features:	The village of Eyam; Eyam Hall and its craft centre (01433 631976); Eyam Museum (01433 631371); Eyam Moor

WALK 23
Chatsworth House

Distance:	13km/8 miles
Start:	Calton Lees car park near Beeley Bridge
Map:	OS Explorer OL24 The Peak District White Peak Area
Terrain:	A fabulous walk through the Chatsworth Estate with a stiff climb from Beeley up to the Rabbit Warren

Chatsworth House is without doubt one of the finest houses in England. It is a magnificent palatial residence which beautifully compliments its majestic setting. The hundred or more acres of formal gardens containing many notable and spectacular features are surrounded by over a thousand acres of sweeping parkland which are set against a glorious natural backcloth of wooded hills with the waters of the River Derwent below. Chatsworth House has long been open to the public and it is also the home of the Eleventh Duke and Duchess of Devonshire. It is affectionately known as the 'Palace of the Peak', a title which it richly deserves.

Bess of Hardwick, who was undoubtedly one of Derbyshire's most profound exhibitionists, built an Elizabethan Chatsworth House in 1555. Bess, daughter of a Derbyshire squire, married four times, each time to a husband more wealthy and influential than the last, and she outlived them all to become the richest and most powerful woman in England after Queen Elizabeth I. Very little remains of the house that Bess built other than the Hunting Tower, which was a gazebo for guests to enjoy the views, and Queen Mary's Bower. Mary Queen of Scots was imprisoned at Chatsworth at various times between 1569 and 1584.

The Fourth Earl of Devonshire attempted to make alterations to Bess's house in the classical manner but the two styles did not mix and he later pulled the house down and built an opulent home on the same site to the latest classical Palladian fashion designs. The house was on a scale befitting the main residence of one of the most prominent aristocratic families in the land with a truly dramatic west front which has become the symbol of Chatsworth. The fourth earl was to become the First Duke of Devonshire. The fourth duke, who was once the prime minister, made great changes to the house and garden. With the help of the architect James Paine new

Chatsworth House

stables were built, the course of the river was altered and a bridge was built. Lancelot 'Capability' Brown was employed to landscape the formal gardens in the natural romantic look which he had brought into fashion.

The sixth 'Bachelor' duke engaged the architect Jeffry Wyatville to construct the long North Wing. He also appointed Joseph Paxton as head gardener cum estate manager in 1826 and he altered the garden into what is seen today, including the dramatic Emperor Fountain which can reach over 85m/280ft. The most famous of Paxton's achievements at Chatsworth was, however, the building of the Great Conservatory. This, in effect, was the forerunner of the Crystal Palace, which he built for the Great Exhibition of 1851 in Hyde Park. Unfortunately the Great Conservatory became derelict during the First World War and was demolished shortly afterwards.

During the Second World War and whilst the tenth duke was in office Chatsworth was closed to the public as it was used by the girls and staff of Penrhos College. The house was not reopened to the public until 1949. The tenth duke's elder son married Kathleen Kennedy, sister of the late President Kennedy, in May 1944. Four months later he was killed in action and Kathleen died in an aeroplane accident in 1948. As they had no children the dukedom passed to the tenth duke's second son, Andrew Cavendish, who is the current duke. Since 1981 Chatsworth has been run by Chatsworth House Trust, a charitable foundation set up by the eleventh duke to preserve the house, its contents, the garden and the park for the benefit of the public.

Emperor Fountain, Chatsworth House

ROUTE INSTRUCTIONS

1 From the car park return to the B6012 and turn right. Immediately after crossing Beeley Bridge turn right through a gate and follow a clear path with the River Derwent over to the right towards Beeley village. Pass through another gate and cross over the road to walk into Beeley, which is a Chatsworth Estate village, with the church on the left. Turn right at a T-junction and then bear right at a fork in a few metres walking towards the Devonshire Arms. Turn left in front of the pub to follow Beeley Brook on the right. Cross over a footbridge and turn left and then walk over another footbridge in 20m and turn right back onto the road.

2 When the road ends and becomes a rough track which bends to the right towards Moor Farm continue ahead along a path with a wall on the left. Climb over a stile on the edge of woodland, now walking with woodland on the right. The route starts to climb uphill and ignores two gates

136

Chatsworth House

that would take you into the wood. When the track runs out climb a stile at the side of a gate into the wood. The path drops downhill with a wall on the left. At a T-junction turn left and cross over a brook. Continue in the same direction, climbing steeply uphill and eventually passing a large flat boulder and later reaching a T-junction. Ignore the footbridge to the right and turn left to follow a track which leads to the edge of the woodland.

3 Climb a stile at the other side of a track that runs by the edge of the woodland onto moorland and follow the broad track, with exceptional views on a clear day across Derbyshire, over an area known as Rabbit Warren. The Warren was once carefully managed by the Devonshires when rabbits were a favourite aristocratic dish. Climb a stile into woodland and follow the path as it bends

to the right. Keep ahead at a crossroad of paths signposted 'Robin Hood' and follow a winding path through woodland, passing first the Swiss Lake on the right and then another lake on the left before the Hunting Tower comes into view. Fifty metres after the Hunting Tower turn right at a signpost for 'Robin Hood'. (The walk may be shortened here by turning left past the Hunting Tower and rejoining the route at Chatsworth Bridge – see map.)

4 After several hundred metres bear left at a concessionary footpath signposted for Baslow, which passes through woodland and out into Chatsworth Park. Walk half left, heading over to a track across the park. Cross over the track and continue in the same direction to another track. Cross this and head towards the surfaced riverside track by the Derwent. Turn left onto this track and follow it, ignoring all offshoots and passing White Lodge and Queen Mary's Bower before reaching Chatsworth Bridge with glorious views of Chatsworth House. Cross over the bridge and turn left onto the riverside fields. After climbing up onto a ridge keep to the ridge top rather than the riverside, making for a small disused building. From here the car park is over to the right.

Refreshments:	Cafe at Calton Lees Garden Centre and the Devonshire Arms pub at Beeley
Toilets:	Calton Lees Garden Centre
Key Features:	Chatsworth Estate including Chatsworth House (01246 582204)

WALK 24
Chatsworth House, Bakewell and Edensor

Distance:	13km/8 miles or 10.5km/6½ miles	
Start:	Calton Lees car park off the B6012 near Beeley Bridge, Chatsworth Park. An alternative starting point is the car park near Bakewell Bridge off Coombs Road.	
Map:	OS Explorer OL24 The Peak District White Peak Area	
Terrain:	An undulating walk between the Chatsworth Estate and Bakewell	

For information on Chatsworth House see Walk 23. For information on Bakewell see Walk 15.

Edensor, pronounced 'Ensor', was built by the Sixth Duke of Devonshire between 1838 and 1842. The duke had the original village, which was much closer to

Edensor from Chatsworth Park

Edensor Church

Chatsworth House, demolished because it spoilt the view. All that remains of the first village is Park Cottage. Unable to decide on a design the duke had all the cottages and houses built in a variety of architectural styles including Swiss and Italian influences, and no two houses are the same. His gardener cum estate manager Joseph Paxton assisted the duke with the designs, along with the Derby architect John Robertson. The Parish Church of St Peter, which dominates the village, was built later in 1867 and as you would expect it contains many monuments to the Cavendish family. Joseph Paxton and Kathleen Kennedy are also buried in the churchyard.

ROUTE INSTRUCTIONS

1 From the car park turn right onto a lane and walk past the entrance to a garden centre on the left. The lane bends to the right to reach a farm. Pass through a gate in front of you onto a rough track and follow the bridleway by a stream to reach Calton Houses. The track bends first to the right and then to the left between the buildings. Continue ahead at a T-junction to reach a gate. After the gate turn left so that you are walking with woodland on your left.

2 The path then bends to the left at the end of the plantation, with another plantation on the right, to a stile by the side of a gate. The track then curves to the right away from the plantation across a field and becomes a path as it heads towards woodland. At a marker post just before the trees, turn right across Calton Pastures. At a corner of the trees maintain direction to a stile by the side of a gate so that you are walking 75m to the right of Manners Wood, passing a tumulus on the right. Head across another long field along a grassy track. Towards the end of the field move over to the right to a gate. Bear left at the fork just after the

gate to walk close to a small plantation, and at the next fork by the plantation turn left to head downhill to a ladder stile into Manners Wood.

3 Scramble down through the wood to a T-junction. Here turn right and then left at a fork in a few metres. Turn right at the next fork, still descending to reach a golf course. Head across the golf course on a grassy track for 50m to climb a stile. Maintain direction to walk over an old railway bridge with the Monsal Trail below. Follow the left-hand edge of a field towards the spire of the church at Bakewell to a small gate onto a track. The track bends to the left to reach Coombs Road with the Agricultural and Business Centre in front of you.

4 Turn right onto Coombs Road and right again at the T-junction with Station Road, unless at this point you wish to explore Bakewell over the town bridge. The road heads uphill and around a left-hand bend. At a fork bear right to cross a bridge back over the Monsal Trail. The old railway station at Bakewell can be seen on the left. Immediately after the bridge bear right onto a bridleway.

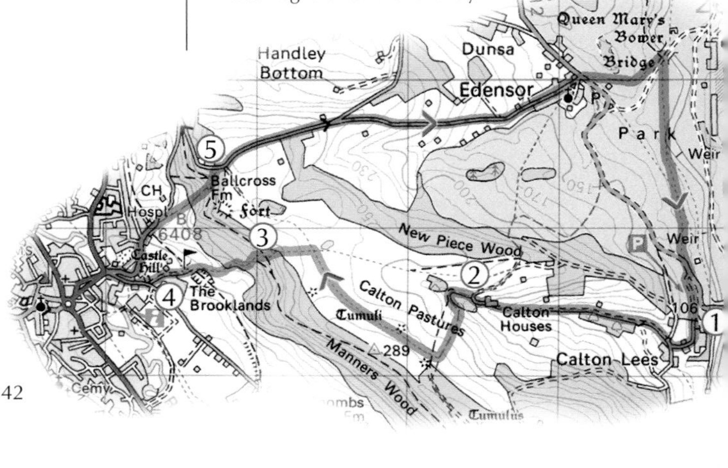

Keep ahead at a crossroads to walk uphill back across the golf course and into Manners Wood. Continue climbing up through the wood to a large T-junction of tracks. Bear left and maintain direction at a crossroads of paths to reach a lane at the edge of the wood just above Ballcross Farm.

5 Turn right onto the lane and then at a fork with the walled rough track bear right. Follow this track, which later becomes a surfaced lane, through the delightful model estate village of Edensor. At the far side of the village cross over the B6012 to the wide gravel track opposite. You are soon rewarded with a magnificent view of Chatsworth House. On reaching Chatsworth Bridge straddling the River Derwent do not cross over the bridge unless you wish to visit the house at this point but turn right to follow the riverside fields back to the car park. After climbing up onto a ridge keep to the top of the ridge rather than the riverside, making for a small disused building. From here the car park is over to the right.

Refreshments:	Calton Lees Garden Centre and a shop at Edensor. A short detour can be made into Bakewell where there are pubs and cafes
Toilets:	Calton Lees Garden Centre
Key Features:	Chatsworth House and its parkland, and the model estate village of Edensor

Distance:	13km/8 miles
Start:	Staunton Harold Reservoir Visitor Centre off the B587 near Melbourne
Map:	OS Explorer 245 The National Forest
Terrain:	A fairly lengthy walk across gentle terrain

Calke Abbey sits hidden away in a hollow within an ancient 750 acre deer park on the Derbyshire/Leicestershire border. It is not an abbey at all but a stately home which was kept as one of the great unknown secrets of Derbyshire until the house came into the hands of the National Trust in 1985 and was opened four years later. Calke represents a unique opportunity to see an English country house in decline, as most have ultimately not survived to tell the tale. It also provides a fascinating insight into the lives of one of England's most eccentric and reclusive families and their passion for natural history.

There has never been an abbey at Calke but an Augustinian Priory was founded on the site in 1130. Today there is no trace of any remains of this religious house, which ceased to function within 50 years. Calke was to become an estate of the Harpur family in 1622, although the family had established itself in Derbyshire in the middle of the previous century. The Baroque mansion was built during 1701–3 by Sir John Harpur to replace his former house at Swarkestone but the identity of the architect remains unclear. Generations of the Harpur Crewe family lived at Calke as virtual recluses in splendid isolation and were content to let the outside world pass them by. Having turned their back on modern life they concentrated their energy on collecting, which has left a spectacular private museum of natural history. The structure of the house may be architecturally unremarkable but Calke's contents are unusually complete. Room after room is filled with cases of antiquities, silver, stuffed birds, toys and minerals.

The house and its contents have stood essentially unchanged since the 1880s as Calke slipped gently from finery to faded glory early in the twentieth century. This untouched time capsule, 'the house that time forgot', has

Calke Abbey (front)

been preserved inside by the National Trust as close as possible to the state in which they found it, including the peeling wallpaper and clutter, though essential repairs were carried out on the structure. Not only were the Harpur Crewes great collectors but they also never threw anything away or sometimes they did not even unpack items. For example, one of the highlights of Calke is the magnificent State Bed with its elaborate brightly coloured Chinese silk hangings which the National Trust found stored in the original crate. Finally, when Charles Harpur Crewe died in 1981, having made no provision to protect the property from death duties and leaving an £8 million tax bill, his brother negotiated the passing of the mansion and its parkland to the National Trust in 1985.

ROUTE INSTRUCTIONS

1 Take the path to the right of the children's play area by the reservoir. Turn left at a T-junction onto a surfaced lane, passing Staunton Harold Sailing Club on the left. At a T-junction turn right

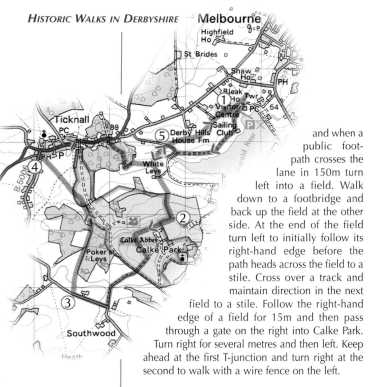

and when a public foot-path crosses the lane in 150m turn left into a field. Walk down to a footbridge and back up the field at the other side. At the end of the field turn left to initially follow its right-hand edge before the path heads across the field to a stile. Cross over a track and maintain direction in the next field to a stile. Follow the right-hand edge of a field for 15m and then pass through a gate on the right into Calke Park. Turn right for several metres and then left. Keep ahead at the first T-junction and turn right at the second to walk with a wire fence on the left.

2 Follow the path round to the right at one end of Mere Pond to walk by the edge of the water. At a T-junction keep ahead to reach a gate. The path then bends to the left up some steps. At a T-junction turn right and at the end of the lake climb a stile. Fifteen metres after the stile turn left through a gate. Walk gently uphill through trees later walking with a fence on the left with views of Calke Abbey. Climb a stile in the fence and turn right to reach a driveway if you are not visiting Calke Abbey at this point. Turn right onto the driveway and when it bends to the right continue ahead through a gate and onto a rough track. The

track follows the left-hand edge of a field to reach a lane. Turn right onto the lane and 75m after Standley's Barn turn right at a public footpath sign.

3 Walk across a field to a stile in the far left-hand corner. Follow the right-hand edge of the next field by woodland. Cross over a stream and climb a stile by a gate immediately after the stream. Continue along the right-hand edge of the next field to a stile. Head through trees for 50m and walk along the right-hand edge of a field to a stile. In the next field Middle Lodge can be seen over to the right along with the entrance driveway. Bear half left to a stile behind a large tree. Leaving Calke Park head across the middle of a field. Climb a stile, cross over a stream and maintain direction towards the church spire at Ticknall to a stile. In the next field walk to a wall corner and then keep the wall on your left to reach the B5006 in Ticknall.

Calke Abbey gardens

4 Turn right to pass the Staff of Life pub and right again at the T-junction with the A514 to walk through the pretty village of Ticknall. Pass the entrance to Calke Abbey and then turn right at a public footpath sign just before a road sign for Staunton Harold Reservoir onto a rough track. At first the track is lined with private dwellings before it heads into woodland. The track bends to the left at the end of the trees and then heads along the left-hand edge of a field away from the trees. Walk through a gap in the field corner and at a marker post part-way across the field turn left to retrace your steps across two fields and a footbridge in between to a lane.

5 Cross over the lane into a field. Head half right across the field and half left in the next field. Follow the right-hand edge of a field to a stile and walk close to a small plantation to another stile. In the next field keep to the right to a hedge corner and then bear half left over to a stile. Walk along the left-hand edge of two fields and head across a final field to a tower at the entrance to the car park. The First Lord Melbourne built this old tower windmill in 1798.

Refreshments:	Staunton Harold Reservoir Visitor Centre, Calke Abbey and pubs in Ticknall
Toilets:	Staunton Harold Reservoir Visitor Centre and Calke Abbey
Key Features:	Staunton Harold Reservoir; Calke Abbey and its park; the village of Ticknall

WALK 26
Swarkestone

Distance:	6.5km/4 miles
Start:	Roadside parking before the church on Church Lane in Barrow upon Trent, just off the A5132 near Swarkestone
Map:	OS Explorer 245 The National Forest
Terrain:	Flat walking country amidst good scenery

The son of James II, James Edward Stewart, known as the Old Pretender, led a failed Jacobite rebellion in 1715 against George I. Later in 1745 his son Charles Edward Stewart, the Young Pretender and affectionately known as Bonnie Prince Charlie, came to Scotland to raise an army to attempt to claim the Crown for his father. At first he experienced success by capturing Edinburgh, and then he crossed the border into England on a march to London. Once in England, however, he was dismayed by

The tiny village of Swarkestone nestles by the side of the often turbulent Trent close to Swarkestone Bridge. Its Church of St James was largely rebuilt in 1876 but the tower and Harpur chapel are fifteenth century and there is a Norman font. The Harpur family once lived at nearby Swarkestone Hall before they moved their country seat to Calke Abbey.

Swarkestone Bridge

149

the lack of support for his cause and chose to retreat on reaching Swarkestone Bridge in Derbyshire. This event has gone down as one of the most momentous in English history because, unknown to Bonnie Prince Charlie, there was total panic in the capital about the advance and, had he decided to continue, it is possible that the course of history would have been dramatically altered.

Swarkestone Bridge also has many other interesting points. It was built during the thirteenth and fourteenth centuries to cross the River Trent and its flood plain, and at nearly a mile/1.5km long, with 17 arches, it is the longest stone bridge in England. For approximately 300 years it was of great strategic importance as it was the main crossing of the River Trent in the Midlands. For example in 1643, during the Civil War, the bridge and causeway were the site of a battle where the Royalists defended the structure by defeating the Cromwellian Sir John Gell from Hopton Hall. This remarkable medieval survivor, which once incorporated a bridge chapel, was much restored during the eighteenth century and now carries the A514 across the river and low-lying meadows. The bridge itself across the river was rebuilt in 1797 and the remains of the demolished bridge are the cause of the rough water seen today below the arches.

Swarkestone Hall was demolished long ago but the 'Summerhouse' or 'Grandstand' still remains. It is thought that John Smythson of the Smythson architectural dynasty, who were responsible for the design of a number of significant properties including Hardwick Hall and Bolsover Castle, built this now rather odd-looking structure for the Harpurs. The exact purpose of the building is unclear but it is thought that it acted as a grandstand and pavilion for a bowling green.

The 150km/93 mile long Trent and Mersey Canal links the Trent at Shardlow with the Mersey at Preston and was designed by the famous canal engineer James Brindley. It was a very important line of communication because for the first time it allowed the direct carriage of goods from the Midlands to either the Humber ports and the North Sea or the Mersey Ports and the Irish Sea.

ROUTE INSTRUCTIONS

1 Follow Church Lane to the pretty Church of St Wilfred. The lane bends to the left by the church and follows the River Trent on the right, passing a number of pleasant properties on the left. At the end of the lane keep ahead on an enclosed footpath by the side of the river. Cross over a footbridge and follow the right-hand edge of a field. In the next field the path heads half left across the field towards trees. Just before the trees the path then bends slightly to the right and then to the left to reach a stile. Climb the stile and follow the grassy winding path to a T-junction close to the riverbank with a first view of Swarkestone Bridge. Turn left and climb a stile at the side of a gate. Turn right on reaching a road to meet the A514 with the Crewe and Harpur Arms, an old coaching inn, on the left and Swarkestone Bridge and causeway to the right.

2 Cross over the road to the path opposite and follow the riverbank, looking back for excellent views of the bridge spanning the Trent, until you reach a T-junction with a lane. Turn left onto the lane and pass the Church of St James in 40m. There is a small open grassy area on the right immediately after the church. Look out for a stile into a field in the far corner of this grass. Climb

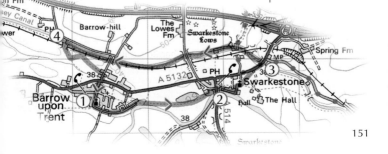

the stile and head diagonally across the field to a stile onto the A5132. As you are crossing this field the 'Summerhouse' of the former Swarkestone Hall is over to the right.

3 Turn right onto the A5132 but do not cross over the road. In 100m just before the Cuttle Bridge bear to the right down to the Trent and Mersey Canal towpath and turn left under the bridge. The towpath soon passes under a railway line to reach Swarkestone Lock. Maintain direction at the lock, passing under Lowes Bridge, Barrow Bridge and then onto Deep Dale Bridge.

4 Leave the canal at Deep Dale Bridge and turn left. A hundred metres after crossing a railway bridge climb a stile on the left and head for a footbridge in the far left-hand corner of the field. Walk across the middle of the next field to

Church of St Wilfred,
Barrow upon Trent

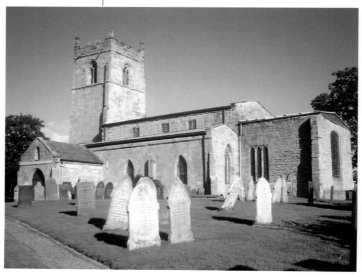

another footbridge. After this footbridge walk to the right of a hedgerow to a stile and then head to the right of a hedge corner to a stile by a metal gate. Turn right onto a lane and cross over the A5132 with care onto Brookfield and back onto Church Lane.

Swarkestone Lock, Trent and Mersey Canal

Refreshments:	Harpur and Crewe pub next to Swarkestone Bridge on the A514 and tea rooms at Swarkestone Lock on the Trent and Mersey Canal
Toilets:	None
Key Features:	The villages of Barrow upon Trent and Swarkestone; Swarkestone Bridge; a section of the Trent and Mersey Canal

WALK 27
Shipley Country Park

Distance:	6.5km/4 miles
Start:	Car park 50m from Shipley Country Park Visitor Centre. Approach the country park from Heanor – it is well signposted from here. Follow the roadway through the park to the car park at the end of the road.
Map:	OS Explorer 260 Nottingham
Terrain:	A slightly undulating walk through Shipley Country Park

In 1976 Derbyshire County Council opened the area as a country park comprising 600 acres of varied landscape and a thousand years of history. The reclaimed spoil heaps are now woodlands, hills and meadows; reservoirs have become peaceful lakes and former railway lines now provide excellent pathways. Part of Shipley Park is also the American Adventure theme park.

The manor of Shipley was recorded in the *Domesday Book* and it passed through the hands of several prominent families before it became the country seat of the Miller-Mundy family in the early eighteenth century. The Miller-Mundys created much of their wealth by exploiting the local coal reserves. They also built Shipley Hall during the eighteenth century on a hilltop with extensive views of the surrounding area. This was not the first house to be built on the site, although it is not known when the earlier residence was constructed.

Shipley became an important coal mining area and when the Miller-Mundy line came to an end in 1922 the Shipley Colliery Company purchased the country estate. Whilst the hall was in the ownership of the Miller-Mundys they had not allowed any coal to be extracted below the hall or its grounds. The Colliery Company, however, soon started to tackle the rich seams and the now derelict hall suffered extensive damage from subsidence and was eventually demolished during the Second World War.

ROUTE INSTRUCTIONS

1 Ignore the signpost to the visitor centre and join a surfaced path by a wooden barrier to walk to the right of the centre. Just after the centre you pass a private property on the left. The path bends to the left and then left again in front of Flatmeadow Farm. Climb a stile and walk along a field edge next to a wire fence. Turn right onto a rough track called Bell Lane and cross over a stream. Immediately after the stream turn left onto a footpath. At a T-junction turn left and cross over the stream. The path bends to the right to walk alongside Mapperley Reservoir.

2 Turn left on reaching a lane at the far end of the reservoir. Pass a car park with toilet facilities on the left and walk up Shipley Lane. Turn right on reaching the edge of woodland on Shipley Hill. At the fork in front of you bear to the right and at the T-junction at the top of a short hill keep ahead. The American Adventure theme park can be seen over to the right. At a crossroad of paths turn left and then turn right at a T-junction. A water tower can be seen over to the left and the site of Shipley Hall to the right. Follow the edge of the site to a large information board and then continue to follow the perimeter until it sweeps left away from the foundations. Turn left at a T-junction and then bear right at the next junction. In 15m turn right to double back on yourself onto Lodge Walk.

3 At a fork bear left onto a bridleway signposted 'The Field'. Follow Dog Kennel Lane down an incline and around a left-hand bend. Again the American Adventure park comes into view including the headgear of

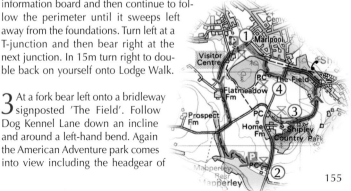

155

the old Mapperley Colliery. The track later becomes a surfaced lane and passes to the right of Shipley Cricket Club. Cross over the road at a T-junction by the Lakeside Business Centre and turn left onto a surfaced bridleway, which was a former railway line. On reaching Osborne's Pond on the left drop down to the pond and follow a surfaced lane along its edge.

4 At the other side turn right onto a path, passing toilet facilities on the left. Take the second path on the left away from the pond. Turn left at a T-junction and then left at a crossroad of paths to arrive back at the car park near the visitor centre.

Refreshments:	Shipley Country Park Visitor Centre
Toilets:	Visitor centre, car park near Mapperley Reservoir and Osborne's Pond
Key Features:	Shipley Country Park and its visitor centre (01773 719961)

Distance:	5km/3 miles
Start:	Kedleston Hall car park
Map:	OS Explorer 259 Derby
Terrain:	An excellent easy walk through the grounds of Kedleston Hall

This walk can only be completed when the park is open (from April to November). Please check opening times before setting off and note that the hall has more restricted visiting hours than the park.

The Curzons came to Britain from Normandy around the time of William the Conqueror. They have probably lived at Kedleston since 1150, although recorded evidence is only available since 1198/99. Their Derbyshire estates grew gradually over the next few centuries and then more rapidly after 1640 due to Sir John Curzon, who also raised the family status by being created a baronet in 1641.

There has been a house at Kedleston since medieval times but it is the second baronet's house, built around 1700, of which there is the first visual record. The second baronet married Sarah Penn, daughter of William Penn, founder of Pennsylvania, so beginning the family's long ties with America. The fifth baronet (later First Lord Scarsdale), Sir Nathaniel Curzon, inherited the Kedleston estate in 1758. He had immediate plans to build himself a new palatial mansion set in beautiful parkland with lakes to rival Chatsworth. He tore down his grandfather's house and moved the nearby village, leaving only the church. After trying out a succession of architects Curzon eventually settled on Robert Adam, a renowned architect

Robert Adam, the famous architect who designed the present neoclassical mansion, created this 5km/3 mile walk known as the Long Walk in the landscaped 820 acre park of Kedleston. The hall, which is now in the hands of the National Trust, is still lived in today (East Wing) by the Curzon family who have had an association with Kedleston for over 800 years.

157

Kedleston Hall

of his day who drew inspiration from the monuments of ancient Rome. The fashionable Pleasure Grounds were also the creation of Adam. The result was a masterpiece of mid-eighteenth-century architecture and is considered to be amongst the finest of Adam's work. The hall has been open to visitors since it was 'finished' in 1765, although it must be borne in mind that the large central block was never intended as a family home. Described as 'an exquisitely designed display cabinet of English eighteenth-century craftsmanship' this part of the house was for grand entertaining as a 'temple of the arts' celebrating one landowner's consuming fascination with classical Rome in the Age of Elegance.

After the First Lord Scarsdale the family led the quiet life of country landowners with the exception of George Nathaniel Marquis Curzon. He had a glittering career which included the posts of Viceroy of India from 1899 to 1905 and Foreign Secretary from 1919 to 1924. His time as viceroy was at the highpoint of the Indian Raj, the climax of which was the Delhi Durbar in 1903 to celebrate the accession of Edward VII. A painting of Lady

Curzon wearing the stunning Peacock Dress, made for her to attend this function and consisting of silk chiffon embroidered with metal threads to look like peacock feathers, is one of the attractions in the hall. The Indian Museum within Kedleston Hall displays many of the gifts Curzon received as viceroy and during his travels of Asia. Whilst acting as foreign secretary Curzon devised the form of Remembrance Day Service that is still used today. George Nathaniel finally inherited Kedleston in 1916, only nine years before his death, but in this time he put considerable energy into vital restoration work. He would today no doubt feel proud that his nephew Viscount Scarsdale arranged for the hall, its contents and the peaceful parkland to come into the administration of the National Trust in 1987.

ROUTE INSTRUCTIONS

1 When driving to the car park you pass Kedleston Hall. Walk back to the hall and pass the front of it to reach the lake. Adam Bridge can be seen over to the left. Turn right by the lakeside. Kedleston golf course and the Sulphur Bath House can be seen on the other side of the lake. Continue by the water's edge after a weir to reach a gate by a 'Long Walk' sign.

2 Shortly after the gate turn right by a weir and cross over a stream. Turn left at a T-junction and follow a wide grassy winding track through young trees. The track later climbs uphill and then turns sharp right onto a tree-lined path with glimpses of Kedleston Hall and Adam Bridge. Pass through a gate and maintain direction to

159

Adam Bridge from Kedleston Hall

another gate in 50m through Vicar Wood. When directly opposite the hall there is a magnificent view of the rear of Kedleston. At a crossroad of paths by a 'Short Walk' sign keep ahead. The path later swings round to the right then to the left and back to the right and leads to the entrance gates to the gardens. Walk with a ditch on the left and turn left at a T-junction of paths. Thirty metres further on pass through a gate on the left back into the car park.

Refreshments:	Kedleston Hall
Toilets:	Kedleston Hall
Key Features:	Kedleston Hall and Park (01332 842191)

WALK 29
Magpie Lead Mine

Distance:	9km/5½ miles
Start:	White Lodge car park on the A6 between Ashford in the Water and Taddington Dale (car park closes at 4pm)
Map:	OS Explorer OL24 The Peak District White Peak Area
Terrain:	A very steep climb out of Deepdale but otherwise a relatively modest degree of difficulty across fields and through woodland

The Magpie Mine has been worked on and off under many different owners for nearly 300 years from around 1682, but like so many other mines in the search for more ore the shafts were driven deeper and deeper until the water table was breached. This meant that flooding then became a constant problem and the future of the mine was always in jeopardy. The impressive and interesting Magpie Mine surface remains stand above shafts running 222m/730ft below the surface. The ruins include a Cornish Engine House with its distinctive round chimney and a square Derbyshire chimney, both dating back to about 1870.

Over time numerous different methods were employed to try to combat the danger of flooding at the Magpie Mine, including the installation of various types of steam-driven pump. As none of these provided an adequate solution a major project was undertaken between 1873 and 1881 at a considerable cost of £18,000 to build a tunnel to drain the water into the River Wye over a mile/1.5km away. This was called the Magpie sough (sough, pronounced 'suff', is the Derbyshire word for a tunnel to drain a lead mine). A final attempt to combat

The Magpie Lead Mine, a Scheduled Ancient Monument and an important site of industrial archaeology, is set on a high windswept plateau near the village of Sheldon. The mine provides the most extensive and best-preserved surface remains of any lead mine in Derbyshire. The stark and evocative ruins are now owned by the Peak District Mines Historical Society, based at Matlock Bath, which uses the site as a field study centre.

the floodwater was made in the early 1950s but this was unsuccessful and the mine finally closed in 1958. In the 1960s, following the collapse of a mineshaft, the sough became blocked and the pressure led to a massive explosion of water in 1966. Magpie Mine's heyday was around 1870 when it employed 50 men and achieved the status of third-largest lead producer in Derbyshire.

Apart from flooding, another common problem in lead mining was disputes over the rights to veins. The Magpie Mine was no exception, especially in the early nineteenth century. The height of tensions was reached in 1833 when opposing miners from the Magpie and Redsoil mines literally met underground. Each was to deliberately set off sulphurous fires to try and smoke out their opponents, which resulted in the deaths of three miners.

The nearby village of Sheldon not surprisingly is a former farming turned lead mining community. Most of its limestone farmhouses and cottages date back to the eighteenth century, as lead mining began to flourish, and the Magpie Mine was to provide the main source of employment for the village.

ROUTE INSTRUCTIONS

1 From the side of the pay and display ticket machine at the back of the car park take the path which leads to a stile in 30m. Climb this stile and then another in 100m. Keep ahead to cross a stream by a marker post for Deep Dale and ignore the path off to the right for Taddington to reach a wall. Walk with the wall on your left to a stile in 50m. Climb the stile and follow the signpost for Ashford, Deep Dale and Sheldon, walking uphill to a junction of paths by a signpost which you will return to near the end of the walk. At this point turn right for Deep Dale and Monyash and follow the path to a wall. Turn left by the wall so that you are walking with the wall on the right through the high-sided valley of Deep Dale with woodland on the right for most of the way for 1 mile/1.5km to a

wall corner. Pass through a gate on the right and turn left to continue up the valley for another 50m, now with the wall on your left to a stile.

2 Climb steeply uphill out of Deep Dale to a stile in a wall. Head across a field with views of the Magpie Mine half right and pass through a gate. Follow the left-hand edge of three fields and in the fourth field maintain direction at the wall corner to a stile. Walk half right across the field corner to a squeeze stile and then walk across the middle of a field to a stile and out onto a lane. Turn left and as the lane bends to the right into Sheldon there is footpath sign for 'Magpie Mine' over to the right. Pass through the gap at the side of a gate next to a signpost and follow a wall on the right to a stile. Climb the stile into a field and maintain direction to a stile in a field corner. Walk along the left-hand edge of the next field to a gap and gate behind it in the field corner to reach a junction of paths. Disregard the track to the left and pass through a gap in front of you into a field and head for the Magpie Mine. Climb a stile and at the fork immediately in front of you bear to the right to reach a stile on the edge of the mine workings. It is free of charge to look around Magpie Mine before returning to this stile.

3 Bear half right to a stile by a marker post just to the right of a gate. Head across a field bearing slightly to the left passing a wall corner and maintaining direction to a footpath sign.

163

Climb a stile next to the signpost and walk across the field picking your way round old lead-mine workings to a stile at the side of gate. Follow a green lane to a road. Turn left onto the road and just before the first building on the right pass through a gap by a public footpath signpost to walk along a valley bottom. At the fork in 30m keep ahead, walking to the right of a large gate to a smaller gate 20m beyond the first gate. Negotiate another gate in 50m to enter woodland.

4 The route drops gently down through Little Shacklow Wood and later bears to the right so that you are walking with conifers on the left to eventually reach a stile. Climb the stile into a field and walk towards the River Wye. Thirty metres before the end of the field bear slightly to the left to a public footpath sign. Turn left in front of the stile, initially walking along a track and then by a wall on the left. Climb a stile at the side of gate to reach a bridge over the Wye by a disused mill. Do not continue straight ahead or cross the bridge but take the path at the back of the mill, soon walking next to the Wye again and passing a weir. By a series of pools the path moves away from the river and follows the edge of Great Shacklow Wood. At a crossroad of paths by a public footpath signpost keep ahead as the path now enters the woodland and runs high above the A6 passing over the outlet to the Magpie Mine sough. Cross a wooden stile in a wall and maintain direction to return to a junction you passed in the early part of the walk. Here turn right to retrace your steps and climb a series of stiles back to the car park.

Refreshments:	None
Toilets:	White Lodge car park. Sign at the rear of the car park near the ticket machine
Key Features:	Magpie Lead Mine

WALK 30
Wirksworth and Middleton Top Engine House

Distance:	8km/5 miles
Start:	Car park on Coldwell Street, Wirksworth, near the Market Place
Map:	OS Explorer OL24 The Peak District White Peak Area
Terrain:	A longish climb up out of Bolehill and to Middleton Top Engine House on the High Peak Trail. Also towards the end of the walk you will be walking along the fenced edge of a quarry. Extra care is required with young children, and dogs should be kept on a lead.

Wirksworth is a small town positioned in a bowl of the surrounding hills whose past prosperity was heavily based on lead mining, even as far back as Roman times, and later quarrying. The Market Place is set at the heart of the town with the Church of St Mary nearby. The church contains one of the most interesting Anglo-Saxon remains in Britain and possibly the Peak District's earliest Christian monument, a coffin lid discovered in 1820 dating from the late seventh century.

Following the collapse of the lead mining industry in the nineteenth century Wirksworth began to decline. Limestone quarrying followed, which did provide employment but the town became badly affected by the resultant dust, dirt and noise, especially after the opening of the Dale Quarry in 1925–26. Fortunately, since the 1980s this decaying town founded on mineral wealth

Wirksworth has a steadily growing tourist trade and is seen as a good base to explore the many local attractions. The story of Wirksworth, its local customs and industries is told in the excellent heritage centre, based in an old silk and velvet mill in the Crown Yard (opposite the Hope and Anchor pub) off the Market Place. Wirksworth also has literary connections as George Eliot (real name Mary Ann Evans) set her first full-length novel *Adam Bede* around 'Snowfield' (Wirksworth), and the area was the home of D H Lawrence for a year.

has been completely transformed with great credit to the local people, which has been recognised by a number of awards. The catalyst was the work by the local Civic Society, the Civic Trust and Derbyshire Historic Buildings Trust.

The Steeple Grange Light Railway is a 450mm gauge line built on the trackbed of a branch line of the Cromford and High Peak Railway and has been restored by enthusiasts to provide a short journey into the disused Dark Lane quarry. Passengers are carried in a man-rider salvaged from Bevercotes Colliery in Nottinghamshire and pulled by a battery-electric locomotive built by Grenwood and Batley Ltd of Leeds. There is also a mining collection of locomotives and rolling stock.

The Middleton Top Engine House is the sole survivor of those that stood at the top of every incline on the Cromford and High Peak Railway to haul wagons up the track and has a fully restored beam winding engine which was built by the Butterley Company of Ripley in 1829. The engine is steamed up on certain Sundays and bank holidays through the summer. Both the house and the engine are a designated an Ancient Monument.

ROUTE INSTRUCTIONS

1 Leave the car park by the top end and turn left into Chapel Lane. The Barmote Court, which was set up in 1288 to enforce mining laws, still sits twice a year at Moot Hall in Chapel Lane. It is almost certainly the oldest industrial court in Britain and possibly the world. Turn left at a T-junction. At the junction with

Black Rocks

the B5036 in a few metres turn right (not onto the
B5036) to walk past Wirksworth infant school on
the left and Wirksworth factory shop on the right.
Cross over an old railway bridge to reach a kissing
gate.

2 Bear left onto a gravel path and follow it across
several fields to a kissing gate. The gravel path
now continues between two wire fences. At a T-
junction with a track turn right. On reaching a
road at Bolehill, cross over to take the uphill path
opposite, passing a Methodist church on the left.
At a crossroads continue ahead on The Lanes.
Look out carefully for a path off to the left by a yellow waymarker on a wall. Follow this path, still
climbing, to reach a road.

3 Turn right onto the road and in 50m turn left by
a public footpath signpost up some steps. Pass
a marker post and head over to a stile by a gate.
Thirty metres further on climb another stile on the
edge of a wood. At a fork bear left to reach a trig
point. Maintain direction and when you come to
a wire fence follow the path around to the left

ignoring other options. At a fork bear right down some steps and then to the left to drop downhill onto the main path to reach the distinctive Black Rocks on the right. This millstone grit outcrop, which has become very popular with climbers, is worth a short detour to the top for a magnificent view over the Derwent Valley. Continue past the rocks for 30m to reach the High Peak Trail by a car park and small visitor centre.

4 Turn left onto the trail, soon passing the Steeple Grange Light Railway. Shortly after this the National Stone Centre can be visited by a short detour on the left. The centre tells the geological and industrial story of stone from prehistoric times

*Middleton Top
Engine House*

to today's modern high-tech processing. The trail then climbs steeply up to the Middleton Top Engine House. Continue past the engine house to reach a junction of tracks.

5 Turn left and then right in 20m by a marker post into a field. Cross over a track in 10m and drop down some steps to a stile. Climb the stile and head across a field to a wall corner and maintain direction with the wall on the left. Pass through a squeeze stile and walk across two fields via stiles to reach a lane. Climb a stile into the field opposite and cross a field to a gap in the wall. Bear half left in the next field and pass through a gap in the field corner and keep close to the left-hand edge of the next field. Climb a stile to walk with a wire fence on the left separating you from a quarry. This path can become a little overgrown in summer. At a wire fence corner 10m from a lane turn left and in 20m pass through a gap between a wall and a wire fence onto a lane. Turn left onto the lane, passing Norbreck Farm on the right. At a T-junction turn left as signposted for Wirksworth. The road winds down to the Market Place with Crown Yard and the heritage centre on the left near the bottom of the hill. Turn left on reaching the B5036 and right in a few metres back onto Coldwell Street.

Refreshments:	Pubs, cafes and heritage centre in Wirksworth, visitor centre at Black Rocks, National Stone Centre and Middleton Top Engine House Visitor Centre
Toilets:	Coldwell Street car park, heritage centre in Wirksworth, visitor centre at Black Rocks, National Stone Centre and Middleton Top Engine House Visitor Centre
Key Features:	Heritage centre in Wirksworth (01629 825225); visitor centre at Black Rocks; Steeple Grange Light Railway (01629 551123); National Stone Centre (01629 825403); Middleton Top Engine House Visitor Centre (01629 823204)

WALK 31
Lathkill Dale and Bradford Dale

The beautiful Lathkill Dale and Bradford Dale are almost unique in Britain in that their rivers both flow entirely through limestone and their water quality is responsible for the formation of an unusual mineral called tufa. Lathkill Dale contains a rich abundance of wildlife and much of the valley is part of the National Nature Reserve.

Distance:	14.5km/9 miles
Start:	Village of Over Haddon, Lathkill Dale car park
Map:	OS Explorer OL24 The Peak District White Peak Area
Terrain:	A long but thoroughly enjoyable walk along riversides and through fields. One short steep ascent out of Lathkill Dale.

Today the Lathkill is one of the country's purest rivers, famed for the range of aquatic life it is able to sustain. As far back as 1676 Izaac Walton, in *The Compleat Angler*, described the Lathkill as 'the purest and most transparent stream that I ever yet saw, either at home or abroad'.

There is also much evidence of Bronze Age man and of later intense lead mining activity. As early as 1288 there is mention of the Mandale Mine, which was worked through to 1851. By 1500 the valley was becoming an important area for lead mining and during the 1770s the London Lead Company was extracting large quantities of ore from this valley. After the closure of the Mandale Mine it was alleged that deposits of a gold-bearing stone had been found, although the source of

Lathkill Dale

the story remains unknown. The Over Haddon Gold and Silver Mining Company was set up to exploit the find but no gold was found and the company quickly collapsed. All lead mining in Lathkill Dale had ceased by 1856.

The Limestone Way runs for 42km/26 miles across limestone uplands from Matlock to Castleton.

ROUTE INSTRUCTIONS

1 Pass to the right of the toilet block out of the car park and turn right onto a lane opposite the Yew Tree tea room. The lane winds downhill into Lathkill Dale. Just before reaching what is often a dry riverbed bear right onto a track, passing a number of caves created by erosion which have provided shelter for early man. After 2.5km/1½ miles climb a stile to continue by the river on a narrower path with now just a scattering of trees on the right instead of the previous dense wood-land. One kilometre further on turn left over a footbridge to begin the climb out of Lathkill Dale.

2 Follow a path through a wooded valley gradu-ally climbing uphill. At a fork bear left and in 30m at a junction climb a stile on the left to join the Limestone Way. Walk steeply up a long flight of steps to reach a gate at the top of the valley. Follow a grassy path across a field. Pass through a kissing gate and maintain direction in the next field to reach another kissing gate. Continue head-ing towards farm buildings and negotiate a kissing gate. Turn left after the gate to reach another gate on the edge of woodland in 50m. Pass through a gate in 30m and then cross over a small field to yet another gate and then another in 20m on the edge of the woodland. The path then bears right to a gate. Cross over a track to follow a grassy path heading towards trees. Climb a stile in a field cor-ner and follow a clear path through woodland to a stile at the end of the trees. Maintain direction

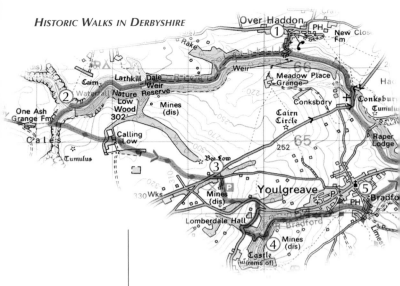

across a field to a stile and continue across a long field towards a line of trees. Climb a stile in a wall and bear half left over to another stile in 20m. Follow the path across a field to reach a lane.

3 Cross over the first lane and take the second, Moor Lane, which is signposted for a picnic site. Immediately after the Moor Lane car park turn right at a public footpath sign. Pass a picnic area on the right to reach a stile by the side of a gate. Maintain direction across a field. As you approach trees the path bends to the left and then starts to drop downhill to a lane. Turn left onto the lane and climb a stile in the wall 50m on the right. Head across a field to a lane and turn right. At the end of a sharp bend look out carefully for a gap in the wall on the left to join a path through a wooded area which winds down into Bradford Dale. When you have almost reached the River Bradford ignore the path that comes in from the left and bear to the right to reach a bridge in 30m.

4 Cross over the bridge and turn left into this magnificent valley bottom passing trout pools which originally provided water to power both corn and lead smelt mills. At a junction of paths pass through a gate and cross over a stone footbridge. Turn right to walk with the river on your right to reach a lane at Alport. Keep ahead on reaching the lane for 20m and then turn left at a T-junction. In 50m opposite Meadows Reach cottage pass through a gate on the right. Follow a grassy ridge with the river now down below on the right to a metal gate. Head across a field to a footpath sign in 75m, at which point the line of the path becomes better defined. Pass between two gateposts and at the fork in front of you bear to the right to reach a road.

5 Cross over the road and then turn right. Turn left at a public footpath signpost for Conksbury to rejoin the River Lathkill, which has met up with the River Bradford nearby. Pass through a squeeze stile to walk along the right-hand edge of a number of fields. Just after Rapers Lodge cross over a track and continue ahead along a clear path to the right to reach a lane. Turn right onto the lane to walk across Conksbury Bridge, an old packhorse bridge, and then turn left immediately after this bridge to follow an exceptional riverside path passing a number of weirs to reach a white house, Lathkill Lodge, where you joined the river near the beginning of the walk. Turn right away from the river to retrace your steps back up a lane to the starting point.

Refreshments:	Craft centre, pub and tea room at Over Haddon
Toilets:	Car park at the starting point
Key Features:	Lathkill Dale; Bradford Dale; the village of Over Haddon

WALK 32
Winster, Elton and
Robin Hood's Stride

Robin Hood's Stride is a spectacular tor of gritstone rock which dominates the skyline. Legend has it that Robin Hood strode between the two large stones at each end. Close by is a Bronze Age stone circle known as Nine Stones, although only four remain today.

Distance:	9km/5½ miles
Start:	The Market House, Winster. Roadside parking in Winster on the B5057
Map:	OS Explorer OL24 The Peak District White Peak Area
Terrain:	A gently undulating walk across fields

Winster's former prosperity, which can clearly be seen in the beautiful sixteenth- and seventeenth-century stone cottages, was based on lead mining and it was also once an important market town. The National Trust purchased

Winster Market House

174

the Market House, built in the late seventeenth or early eighteenth century, in 1906 and this represented their first acquisition in Derbyshire. The property has now been restored and houses a National Trust information room. Including the Market House there are 60 listed buildings in Winster.

The village of Elton is a Peak District village whose former wealth was built on lead mining, and most of the cottages were built by the lead miners during the seventeenth and eighteenth centuries.

ROUTE INSTRUCTIONS

1 From the Market House walk along the B5057 through Winster towards the church. Ten metres before the road bends to the right at a T-junction there is a public footpath sign between buildings on the right. Cross over a track and pass through a farmyard. Head across a field to a small marker post next to a large sycamore tree. Pass through a gate 10m further on to enter woodland. In 20m, just before a stile, bear right at a fork and at the next fork bear left and walk across a field to a stile at the side of a small ruined building. Maintain direction in the next three fields and then pass through a gap in a hedge next to a public footpath sign in the fourth field. Walk half right uphill to a gate and out onto Birchover Lane.

2 Turn right onto the lane and just after the brow of the hill turn left at a public footpath sign. Follow the left-hand edge of fields with Birchover Wood on the left and glimpses of Robin Hood's Stride in the distance. Maintain direction for a while and then walk half right over towards a wall. Keep the wall on your right to pass Rocking Stone Farm and later walk with a wall on the left to a gate. With a wire fence on the left head downhill to a T-junction. Turn right and then in 10m climb a stile on the left to drop down to the B5056.

3 Turn left onto the road and then right onto a lane in 125m. Climb a stile on the right in 20m to join a private drive on the Limestone Way. Follow this rough track uphill towards Robin Hood's Stride and Hermit's Cave, which is opposite the tor. When the track bends to the right keep ahead towards the rock formation. Ignore the fork just before the rock to reach a gap at the side of a gate. Pass Robin Hood's Stride and in 30m just before a gate climb a stile on the left. Climb another stile on the right in 20m into a field. The Nine Stones stone circle can be seen over to the right. There is also a standing stone closer to you. Walk diagonally across two fields to reach a lane by Harthill Moor Farm, which is built on the site of an Iron Age fort.

4 Turn right onto the lane with views of Stanton Hall, the seat of the Thornhill family, over to the right and the church of Stanton in the Peak just behind it. Before the lane bends to the left, turn left by a public footpath sign into a plantation. Follow the clear path through the trees, which later bends to the left to reach a stile at the edge of the plantation. Maintain direction across a field to a gate. After the gate turn left to leave the Limestone Way. Pass through a squeeze stile and walk across the middle of a field towards Tomlinson Wood. The path skirts the edge of the wood on your left. At a public footpath signpost turn sharp right across the field. Pass through a squeeze stile and head across a long field with a plantation on the left and then along the edge of a field with Cliff Farm on the right. Walk across two fields to a wall corner and then keep the wall on your left to a squeeze stile onto a lane.

5 Cross over Cliff Lane to the footpath opposite. Follow a path through fields, passing through gaps in the wall to begin the ascent towards Elton. At the top of the hill turn left by a public footpath sign next to a house. Pass through a gap at the side of a gate onto a rough track. Turn right and then left onto the main street through Elton, passing the Duke of York. Continue on after the village to the T-junction with Dudwood Lane. Turn right onto a track. Leave the track by the driveway to Westhill Farm. Cross over the driveway and negotiate a squeeze stile by a public footpath sign. Walk across the field to a squeeze stile, then along the left-hand edge of a field and the middle of the next field to the B5056. Join a footpath on the opposite side of the road and maintain direction across fields to reach the churchyard at Winster. Walk through the churchyard and turn left onto a lane. At the T-junction turn right to return to the Market House.

Refreshments:	Pubs in Winster and a pub and tea shop in Elton
Toilets:	Winster, on a side street near Market House
Key Features:	The villages of Winster with its Market House (01335 350245) and Elton, and Robin Hood's Stride

WALK 33
Carsington and Brassington

The villages of Carsington and Brassington, like many of the Peak District villages, once depended heavily on lead mining for revenue, and the whole area of this walk is pock-marked by old lead mines and limestone quarries.

Distance:	9.5km/6 miles
Start:	Roadside parking in Carsington village off the B5035 near Carsington Water
Map:	OS Explorer OL24 The Peak District White Peak Area
Terrain:	Trail and field walking with a steep descent back into Carsington

Carsington consists of a line of attractive cottages and the Parish Church of St Margaret with Carsington Pasture rising steeply behind. Although its location remains a mystery, many archaeologists believe Carsington to be the site of Lutaderum, the Roman administrative lead centre. Carsington Reservoir, which is owned by Severn Trent Water, was opened in 1992 by the Queen. Most of the Peak District reservoirs gather water from acid moorland so they are low in nutrients, which affects the level of aquatic plant and animal life they can support. Carsington is different in this respect and attracts numerous birds and wildlife. The award-winning visitor centre on the site follows the journey of water from the reservoir to the tap through interactive displays, and numerous activities can be pursued including waterborne sports, birdwatching, cycling and walking.

Brassington is another pretty limestone village which sits on a hillside and is made up of largely seventeenth- and eighteenth-century houses and a Norman church with Saxon remains. A Roman road called The Street once ran through the village.

ROUTE INSTRUCTIONS

1 Walk through the village of Carsington in the direction of Brassington and when the road

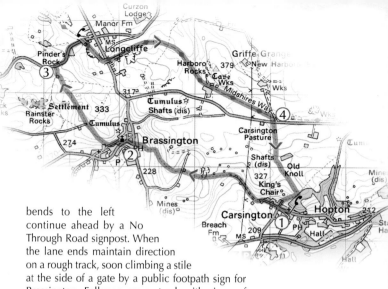

bends to the left
continue ahead by a No
Through Road signpost. When
the lane ends maintain direction
on a rough track, soon climbing a stile
at the side of a gate by a public footpath sign for
Brassington. Follow a grassy track with views of
Carsington Reservoir on the left. Climb a stile at
the side of a gate and at the fork immediately in
front of you bear to the right. Keep ahead at a
crossroad of paths and continue to a stile. Walk
across a field and pass through a squeeze stile
onto a track. Pass through another squeeze stile at
the other side of the track onto a grassy track. In
75m at a fork bear left and soon start to drop
downhill towards the village of Brassington. Pass
through a squeeze stile and in 100m turn left
through another squeeze stile. Follow the right-
hand edge of a field, still dropping downhill, to a
squeeze stile in the wall on the right. Head across
a field, moving ever closer to Brassington, and
negotiate a squeeze stile in a hedge. In the next
field make for the far left-hand corner and some
steps. Walk by a wall on the left through a farmyard to a road junction.

2 Cross over the junction to walk past Dragon
Cottage on the right and the Miners Arms on

*Carsington Water from
Carsington Pasture*

the left. Follow the road round to the left by the pub, with St James's Church on the right. Opposite Ye Olde Gate Inn, built in 1616 on a former turnpike road, turn right along an alleyway. At a junction of paths turn right to reach a lane. Turn right onto the lane and then in 20m turn left by a public footpath sign through a squeeze stile. The path bears to the left and heads uphill to another squeeze stile. Continue along the grassy track and as you reach the top of the hill Rainster Rocks can be seen over to the left. This rock formation is an example of dolomitic limestone. Pass through a squeeze stile onto a track and cross over the track to enter a field. Maintain direction close to the edge of a ridge to pass through a large gap in a wall near the far left-hand corner of the field. Head half right across the next field to a squeeze stile 10m to the right of the field corner. Drop downhill towards disused farm buildings, passing between two gateposts. Twenty metres further on pass through a squeeze stile in front of you. Keep to the left of the farm buildings to reach a track and turn right onto it.

3 Turn right onto the B5056. After several hundred metres pass under an old railway bridge and 20m after the bridge turn right through a gap in a wall by a signpost for the High Peak Trail. Follow a lane past the station shop on the left to soon reach the High Peak Trail. Turn left onto the

Harborough Rocks

trail. Pass above a minor road and keep ahead at two crossroads of paths to eventually reach Harborough Rocks on the left. This is another example of dolomitic limestone; it is now popular with climbers but was once the home of prehistoric man. Continue along the trail until you are about 20m away from a lane. Here climb a stile on the right by a public footpath sign for Carsington and cross over a small field to reach the lane.

4 Cross over the lane and enter Carsington Pasture. Walk by a wall on the left first dropping downhill and then climbing back up. At the top of the hill Carsington Reservoir comes back into view. Remain close to the wall on the left, heading towards trees and passing a rock formation on the left, which is on private land, called the King's Chair. Ten metres before reaching the trees turn right onto a footpath which drops steeply down towards Carsington. Pass through a gate and down some steps. Keep ahead to reach a lane. Turn left and retrace your steps to the starting point.

Refreshments:	Pubs in Carsington and Brassington and at the station shop just before joining the High Peak Trail
Toilets:	None
Key Features:	The villages of Carsington and Brassington; Carsington Pasture; a section of the High Peak Trail

WALK 34
Cromford

Distance:	9.5km/6 miles
Start:	Cromford Wharf car park, Mill Lane/Road, Cromford
Map:	OS Explorer OL24 The Peak District White Peak Area
Terrain:	After an initial climb out of Cromford this is an easy walk with plenty of variety

Cromford is hugely important in world history terms, along with other mill complex sites in the Derwent Valley, as the cradle of the Industrial Revolution. What makes Cromford so special is that not only was it the first but it is also a rare remaining example of an early Industrial Revolution textile settlement and, unusually, many of the original buildings and features remain. Richard Arkwright's contribution in establishing Cromford as the birthplace of the techniques of mass production has earned him the accolade 'Father of the Factory System'.

In 1771 Richard Arkwright went to Cromford and, in partnership with Jedediah Strutt and Samuel Need, established the world's first successful water-powered cotton spinning mill and built around it the first custom-built industrial community, which became a model for others throughout the world. As a benevolent employer this included good quality housing by the standards of the day and social provisions. He soon built a second and much larger mill at Cromford in 1777, which became the basic design for factories for the next 150 years, although this mill was destroyed by fire in 1890. His third mill at Cromford was the showpiece red-brick Masson Mill which he constructed at the height of his entrepreneurial power in 1783. Arkwright was rewarded in 1786 for his achievements by becoming the first ever commoner to be knighted and a year later he became High Sheriff of Derbyshire.

It was the success of the new factory system that stimulated the demand for more efficient communications, which led Arkwright and others to promote construction of the Cromford Canal, which was completed in 1794. The engineer was William Jessop in partnership with Benjamin Outram and the total cost of the project was £80,000. The canal provided a vital artery into the national canal network and was the first part of a link from the Midlands to the North West. The 23km/14½ mile canal ran from Langley Mill on the Erewash Canal, which joined the River Trent, to its northern terminus at Cromford Wharf. As a whole the canal was very busy and profitable, latterly carrying mainly coal and limestone. Eventually Derbyshire County Council purchased the section of the canal from Cromford to Ambergate and developed it for recreational purposes.

Leawood Pump House was built in 1849 to lift water from the River Derwent to maintain a consistent level of water in the canal. It is now a listed building which has been fully restored with its Watt-type beam engine. Nearby is the Wigwell, or Derwent, Aqueduct as it is also known. This listed building carries the canal across the river on an arch with a 24m/80ft span.

The construction of the Cromford and High Peak Railway was considered an engineering masterpiece, which later attracted railway enthusiasts from all over the world. Engineered by William Jessop's son Josiah and opened in 1831, canal principles were clearly demonstrated in its construction, with locks substituted by steam-powered beam engines to haul wagons up the

Lea pumping station, Cromford Canal

steep inclines. Initially horses were used to haul the wagons up the long steep gradients. The horses were replaced by locomotives in 1832 but it was still an arduous 16 hour journey to complete the 53km/33 miles, including the steepest locomotive-worked gradient of any British railway, the 1 in 14 Hopton Incline. Some passengers were carried along with the bulk cargoes but the passenger service was terminated in 1872. A catch pit was later built at Sheep Pasture Incline which can still be seen today, along with interesting railway workshops, memorabilia and a visitor centre at High Peak Junction. After the railway's closure in 1967 the trackbed from High Peak Junction to Dowlow near Buxton was converted by Derbyshire County Council and the Peak National Park Authority into the enormously popular 28km/17½ mile High Peak Trail.

Cromford's relatively poor communications led to an end to textile production at Cromford Mill around 1840. The buildings were then used for a variety of industries including brewing, laundries, cheese warehousing and finally in the early twentieth century for the production of colour pigments for paints and dyes. The site was finally abandoned in 1979, heavily contaminated with lead chromate. The same year the Arkwright Society bought Cromford Mill and extensive work has since followed. The site is now a major tourist attraction with guided tours and shops. Masson Mill was the oldest mill in the world in continuous production until 1991. In 1999 it opened to the public as a working textile museum and shopping village.

ROUTE INSTRUCTIONS

1 From the car park return to Mill Road. Over to the right is St Mary's Parish Church where Sir Richard Arkwright is buried. Turn left with views of Willersley Castle, now a hotel, over to the right. Arkwright built this grandiose mock Gothic property, which is a frequent feature of this walk, but he died in 1792 before it was completed. Whilst Arkwright was at Cromford he lived at Rock House which is set up on the clifftop opposite his mills. Pass the Cromford Mill complex on the right and walk under the cast iron aqueduct to the A6. Cross over the A6 and head up towards Cromford village. Turn right in front of the Greyhound Hotel built by Arkwright and walk alongside a millpond with a working mid-nineteenth-century waterwheel. Turn left at a T-junction to return to the Market Place. Turn right up The Hill and note the fine three-storey gritstone houses along North Street built by Arkwright. After North Street turn left onto Bedehouse Lane and in 20m bear right onto a walled uphill path with views of the striking millstone grit outcrops of Black Rocks – these are popular with climbers and offer excellent views of the Derwent Valley ahead.

2 Continue until you reach a road. Cross over the road and keep ahead on a path signposted to Black Rocks. Turn left at a T-junction onto a track and follow it as it bends to the right, still heading up towards the rocks. At a T-junction which is signposted for the Black Rocks and High Peak Trail turn left. Pass through a gap at the side of a gate into woodland. The path bends to the right in front of a stile onto the High Peak Trail. Turn left onto the trail, passing Sheep Pasture Engine House which once housed a stationary steam-winding engine on the right before beginning to drop down the 1 in 8 Sheep Incline. Continue ahead at the crossroads with the Midshires Way and then turn right through a gate into Birch Wood.

3 Walk along the clear path through the wood, eventually passing through a squeeze stile at the side of a gate by farm buildings. At a fork in the track bear to the left but when the track bends to the right onto a private road keep ahead through woodland. The path moves ever closer to the A6 and leads to a T-junction. Turn left and then right in a few metres to walk to the A6. Crich Stand at nearly 300m/985ft above sea level sits prominently on top of a limestone quarry ridge in the distance. This 19m/62ft beacon tower was erected in 1923 as a

Cromford village pond

Crich Stand

war memorial to the Sherwood Foresters in the First World War. Cross over the road with care onto a driveway by a public footpath signpost. The path soon bends to the left and under a railway bridge. Cross a footbridge over the River Derwent and turn left. In a few metres bear right at a fork onto a path which soon leads to the Cromford Canal towpath. Gregory Tunnel is to the right but your route turns left along a delightful stretch of canal. Just before the Leawood Pump House turn right over a bridge. If you wish to visit High Peak Junction cross over the next swing bridge, but otherwise continue ahead to return to Cromford Wharf.

Refreshments:	Arkwright's mill, pubs in Cromford, the Homesford Cottage Inn at Whatstandwell on the A6 and the information centre at High Peak Junction
Toilets:	Cromford Wharf car park and High Peak Junction
Key Features:	Arkwright's Cromford Mill (01629 824297); Arkwright's Masson Mill (01629 581001); Arkwright's model village of Cromford; Black Rocks; a section of the High Peak Trail; a section of the Cromford Canal including Leawood Pump House (open and fully working on occasional weekends through the summer – 01629 823204); High Peak Junction workshops/information centre (01629 822831)

WALK 35
Pinxton Wharf

Pinxton is a former mining village and Pinxton Wharf was the terminus of the Pinxton Arm of the Cromford Canal. The wharf has now been restored and the reclamation process around the route of the canal continues.

Pinxton Wharf

Distance:	4km/2½ miles
Start:	Roadside parking at Pinxton Wharf
Map:	OS Explorer 269 Chesterfield & Alfreton
Terrain:	A flat and very easy walk

The Pinxton Arm of the Cromford Canal was constructed to provide a link to the River Trent via the Erewash Canal. The canal primarily carried coal from the many small collieries in the Upper Erewash Valley and pottery from the Pinxton works. The local Coke family started a pottery, producing the now rare and famous highly decorative Pinxton china. It had been intended to continue the canal to link the Mansfield area to the waterways net-

work, however the number of locks that would have been required to raise the canal to the Kirkby Summit made the project impossible. A tramway was later built over Kirkby Summit to Portland Wharf in Mansfield and horses hauled up freight. In the 1830s a small horse-drawn tramway ran every Thursday from the Boat Inn to Mansfield market and it can claim to be the first passenger railway station in Derbyshire.

In the late 1890s the Pinxton Canal began to suffer from a lack of water as a result of coal mining subsidence. As a result the Pinxton to Pye Bridge section could not be navigated. The length between Pye Bridge and the junction with the main body of the Cromford Canal at Ironville remained in use until the 1930s for the transportation of chemicals. The chemical company apparently preferred this method of transport because few breakages were incurred.

ROUTE INSTRUCTIONS

1 From the Wharf walk along either side of the canal to reach the Boat Inn on the left. Shortly after the Boat Inn you reach a track. Continue ahead, still walking with the canal on your right, to a stile at the side of a gate. The route does not follow the line of the public footpath on the OS map as this area is being reclaimed. Head over to the gates of a scrapyard but do not enter it. Instead take the path to the left to walk with a wire fence on the left. The path bends to the left in front of a railway line. On reaching a bridge under the railway line turn right to pass under the bridge onto a track and return to the route of the map.

189

2 Follow the track with a spring on the right and pass under another railway bridge before reaching a lane. Turn right onto the lane and cross over a railway line. When the lane bends to the left climb a stile on the right by a signpost for Pinxton. The path runs between a line of trees. In 75m climb a stile on the left into a field. Keep to the right-hand edge of the field to a stile onto a road. Climb the stile at the other side of the road and turn right onto a public bridleway.

3 The path first bends to the left and then bends to the right into more open countryside. After a short surfaced area turn right with a small pond on the left and in 20m turn left at a T-junction. Cross over a stream and head uphill. The track bends right and then left so that you are now walking with a railway line on the right. At a fork keep ahead and then at the next fork bear to the right to reach a road. Maintain direction to pass Pinxton Longwood infant school and turn right onto Alexander Terrace. Cross over the railway line to return to the starting point.

Refreshments:	Boat Inn on Pinxton Canal
Toilets:	None
Key Features:	Pinxton Wharf

WALK 36
Shardlow

Distance:	5km/3 miles
Start:	Shardlow Wharf car park, Wilne Lane, Shardlow
Map:	OS Explorer 260 Nottingham
Terrain:	A flat and very easy walk along a canal towpath and riverside

Shardlow rose from obscurity as a small farming community with the coming of the Trent and Mersey Canal, built between 1766 and 1777. The canal enabled this insignificant village to rapidly transform itself into an important inland port with storage and distribution facilities and a range of canal associated trades such as smiths, rope makers, and boat and crane builders. As a result the population of Shardlow quadrupled between 1788 and 1841.

The Trent and Mersey Canal, as its present name suggests, links the River Trent with the River Mersey, although its engineer, James Brindley, originally called it the Grand Trunk Canal. This was because the canal provided a means of transporting goods from the west to the east of England and Brindley had future plans for extending the canal with branch links, which never came to fruition. The

Shardlow is one of the best-preserved inland ports in the country which survives largely intact, so it provides plenty of historical interest. The wharf has been protected as a conservation area since 1978, and Shardlow Heritage Centre is housed in a former salt warehouse which stands in the car park of the Clock Warehouse pub. The name of this pub, built in 1780, gives away its former use, and a spur of the canal can still be seen as it enters the warehouse through an arch.

Trent and Mersey Canal

Clock Warehouse pub, Shardlow

main impetus behind the building of the canal was Josiah Wedgwood and the other Staffordshire potters who, until the building of the canal, had faced severe transport problems for their raw materials and finished goods. Once complete the 93 mile/150km route of the canal with 76 locks connected the ports of Liverpool and Hull via the River Mersey through the salt mining area of Cheshire and the Staffordshire Potteries to the River Trent, which leads to the Humber. The ports of Liverpool and Hull acted as vital centres for imported and exported goods all over the world and hence the significance of the Grand Trunk Canal can clearly be seen.

Shardlow was a mile/1.5km from the southern end of the canal and was chosen as the transhipment point where goods were interchanged from the broad river barges to the canal narrowboats. This eighteenth-century inland port bustled with activity for over a hundred years until, as always, the coming of the railways rapidly changed the distribution channels. In its heyday, as one of the major inland ports in England, Shardlow attracted many merchants who made their fortunes and built themselves grand Georgian houses in the village.

ROUTE INSTRUCTIONS

1 Turn right out of the car park onto Wilne Lane. Just before a bridge over the canal walk down some steps on the left onto the towpath. Turn right

to walk away from Shardlow, soon passing Chapel Farm Wharf and the Derwent Mouth Lock. The route takes you across a large footbridge over the River Trent.

2 Immediately after the bridge turn right onto a broad track by the River Trent. Just before a large T-junction of tracks look out for a yellow waymarker on the right to follow a grassy path close to the riverbank. Cross over a small concrete bridge and pass under a sewage pipe. Opposite the entrance to Shardlow Marina the path turns left away from the river so that you are walking with the wall of an old mill on the right.

3 Climb a stile out onto a road junction and turn left and right in a few metres onto the A6. Turn right and cross over the river to walk through Shardlow, passing the Navigation Inn, and cross over Wilne Lane to reach a bridge over the canal. Fifty metres further on are the Shardlow Heritage Centre and the Clock Warehouse pub, both of which are well worth a visit. Turn right onto the towpath and walk along Shardlow Wharf to the bridge where you joined the canal in 150m. Leave the canal at this point and retrace your steps to the starting point.

Refreshments:	Pubs in Shardlow
Toilets:	None
Key Features:	The historic inland port of Shardlow; the Shardlow Heritage Centre (01332 793368); a section of the Trent and Mersey Canal

WALK 37
Belper

Distance:	9.5km/6 miles
Start:	Belper River Gardens long-stay car park off the A6 next to East Mill
Map:	OS Explorer 259 Derby
Terrain:	Apart from a stiff climb out of Belper and on the return leg out of Milford, this is otherwise an easy walk

Belper on the River Derwent grew from a tiny village to a bustling industrial town as pioneering entrepreneurs harnessed the waterpower of the fast-flowing river during the textile revolution. England's 'hardest working river' helped the Derwent Valley become the cradle of the Industrial Revolution, and the route of the Derwent has now been designated the National Heritage Corridor.

The River Derwent is the link in a chain of attractions and Belper is the home of the Derwent Valley Visitor Centre which is a key element of the National Heritage Corridor. The visitor centre is located in part of the historic North Mill. The mill is now recognised as one of the most significant industrial buildings in the world.

Belper is shown in the *Domesday Book* as Beaurepaire, meaning the Beautiful Retreat, and the estate was given by William the Conqueror to the De Ferrers family who created a deer park around the handful of houses scattered by the village green. Over time local coal

North Mill, Belper

and iron resources were exploited to provide the raw materials for domestic industry and Belper gradually gained a reputation and became a major nail producer.

Two dynasties dominated the growth of the textile industry on the River Derwent. One was headed by the famous Richard Arkwright (see Walk 34) and the other family was influenced by Jedediah Strutt, a Derbyshire man who made his first fortune from the development of ribbed knitting. In all, over a period of 40 years, Strutt and his sons built eight mills at Belper and a mill at Milford, south of Belper. Belper expanded rapidly from a rural village with a population of 550 around 1770 to 10,000 by 1840, making it the largest town in the county. The workforce had been transformed from cottage industry nail makers and framework knitters to factory-based cotton spinners, with the Strutts as the major employer controlling every aspect of their working life.

Production began in the North Mill in 1778 but in 1803 it suffered the same fate as many other early timber-framed cotton mills and was burnt to the ground as fire spread rapidly through them. William Strutt, son of Jedediah and an engineer of considerable ability, built the second North Mill in 1804, which still stands today. This iron-framed mill, which also incorporated brick arch floors and a heating system, was one of the world's first fire-resistant buildings and has been described as one of the 'most sophisticated, beautiful and technologically advanced buildings of its era'. It is now the second oldest fireproof iron-framed building in the world. As the forerunner of today's enormous steel-framed structures the value of this monument in industrial archaeology terms can be fully appreciated.

Production continued in the North Mill and the adjoining South Mill until 1912 at which time it was replaced by the present East Mill. Today the North Mill is the setting for the Derwent Valley Visitor Centre which includes a museum highlighting the importance of the industrial heritage of the mills to the growth of the surrounding area. It also, through a common heritage, illustrates the links between Belper and Rhode Island in

For more than 150 years the **Strutt family,** as strict Unitarians, were great benefactors to the town and, at least in the context of the early nineteenth century, they were model employers, providing not only work but housing, education and good food from model farms. Evidence of the family's influence on the town will be seen on the return leg of the walk through Belper. The work was hard and disciplined, but as benevolent employers the Strutts dealt with punishment through a system of fines, and corporal punishment was strictly forbidden. Arguably the Strutts, although less well known than the pioneering Arkwrights of Cromford, have made a greater contribution in the course of history as they revolutionised →

← the construction of textile mills, their factories were far better equipped than Arkwright's and their social provisions were ahead of the time.

America and follows the development of the cotton spinning industry as a whole.

ROUTE INSTRUCTIONS

1 Turn right out of the car park onto the A6 and right again in 50m onto Bridge Foot. The East Mill, a distinctive landmark for miles around, is in front of you and you soon walk under the arches which connected the mill complex on both sides of the road. Strutt took the precaution of building narrow slits into the arches to position guns. Although these defences were never used at Belper 'Trouble at t'mill' from Luddites was not unusual in the early nineteenth-century cotton industry. The Derwent Valley Visitor Centre is on the right in the North Mill. The big heavy entrance doors to the visitor centre were taken from the West Mill which is now demolished. As you cross over the Derwent the spectacular horseshoe weir can be seen, another illustration of a remarkable engineering feat of its time by the Strutts. There is a viewing area at the other side of the bridge. Immediately after crossing over the Derwent turn left onto a surfaced path. When the surfaced path ends continue ahead into a field through a gap next to a small building. Pass through a squeeze stile and then continue onto the next squeeze stile by a gate. Keep ahead along a broad grassy track

River Gardens next to East Mill

leading back towards the riverbank but look out
for a squeeze stile next to a gate over to the right.

2 Bear left for 50m to pass through a squeeze stile
in a hedge and then in the next field walk to the
top right-hand corner to pass through yet another
squeeze stile. Continue half left along a clear uphill
path, making for the corner of a high garden wall.
Just around the wall corner is a stile which leads to
a lane. Turn left onto the lane and in 100m at a public footpath sign on the right pass through a squeeze
stile into a field. Walk along the right-hand edge of
the field and maintain direction in the next field,
climbing uphill more steeply to reach a wide track
at the top of the ridge.

3 Turn left onto the walled North Lane
along a section of the Midshires
Way which gives extensive views of
the Derwent Valley. This prehistoric route was used to avoid
the swampy and densely
forested valley and was
known by the Saxons as the
Portway. After following the
ridge top for 1.5km/1 mile the
track starts to gradually drop
downhill as its passes through
Chevin golf course. Keep
ahead at a T-junction to leave
the Midshires Way, later passing a ventilation tower for the
Milford Tunnel on the left. The
track becomes a surfaced lane
and drops steeply down through
housing to a T-junction. Cross over
the T-junction and walk down Chevin
Alley to the A6 with the Strutt Arms hotel
on the right.

4 Turn left, passing Milford Mill, and cross over the Derwent. Strutt built the first cotton mill at Milford, although this no longer stands. As the road bends to the left turn right in front of the Milford Inn noting the double weir on the river and passing an entrance to the Riverside Garden Centre. Turn left onto a lane signposted for the 'Holly Bush Inn' opposite the Makeney Hotel. Just before reaching the inn turn left up a lane by a public bridleway sign. Continue ahead when the surfaced lane ends and climb steadily up Dark Lane to eventually emerge by Bownsgreen Farm. Turn left onto a track and follow it to Shaw Lane.

5 Turn left onto the lane and immediately after passing through a small wooded area climb some steps on the right to follow a wall on the right. Pass through a squeeze stile at the corner of woodland and walk along the left-hand edge of fields to arrive at a fork at the edge of woodland. Bear right to walk with the woodland on your left to climb a stile in front of Wildersley Farm 20m after the end of the woodland. Turn left onto a track and follow it to a road. Turn right onto the road and when the road bends to the right turn left onto a surfaced path which runs through housing. When the housing ends continue ahead, aiming for the corner of wire

Horseshoe Weir at
Belper

fencing where the path becomes surfaced again and drops downhill. This time, when the surfaced path ends at a fork, head down through woodland briefly and then walk behind goalposts. Immediately after the goalposts turn right and then left at the other side of a hedge to walk past the end of a row of houses. Turn right on meeting a surfaced path and cross a stream to emerge onto New Breck Road.

6 Turn left and immediately right and then right again at a T-junction in 40m. Then turn left in 30m onto King Street and turn right opposite the War Memorial Gardens onto Green Lane. As you cross over Church Lane, St Peter's Church can be seen to the right. This church is of Norman origins but was heavily restored by the Victorians. Shortly afterwards you pass the Congregational Church and Joseph Street is on the left. One of the last surviving and best-preserved nail shops can be seen on the right as a monument to the old cottage industry. As you pass George Street on the left Short Row can be seen. Jedediah Strutt named three streets in Belper after his sons William, Joseph and George. Short Row dates from around 1788 and provided one-up one-down terraced housing. As Green Lane bends to the right continue ahead on the cobbled Long Row. This later development provided much larger two-up two-down terraced houses. At the end of Long Row turn right onto the A6, soon returning to the starting point.

Refreshments:	Shops, cafes and pubs at Belper, Derwent Valley Visitor Centre and a pub and Riverside Garden Centre at Milford
Toilets:	Derwent Valley Visitor Centre and on the A6 virtually opposite East Mill
Key Features:	Derwent Valley Visitor Centre (01773 880474) and the influence of the Strutt family on the lives of the people of Belper and Milford. Belper River Gardens are also worth a visit.

WALK 38
Monsal Head, Litton and Cressbrook

Cressbrook Mill, a magnificent Georgian building which has recently been renovated, looks more like a country house than a mill, with its fine clock and cupola top containing a bell, which would have struck the order of the day. Undoubtedly this is one of the best remaining examples of a Georgian cotton mill in the country, earning admiring glances for both its architecture and wonderful setting. It was a combination of the Litton and Cressbrook mills which Walt Unsworth used as the setting for his children's novel *The Devil's Mill*, first published in 1968.

Distance:	9.5km/6 miles
Start:	Long-stay car park behind the hotel at Monsal Head on the B6465 between Ashford in the Water and Wardlow
Map:	OS Explorer OL24 The Peak District White Peak Area
Terrain:	An undulating and very rewarding walk

As part of his developing empire Richard Arkwright of Cromford established a three-storey cotton-spinning mill in 1779 on the site of a former peppermint distillery at Cressbrook. The distillery had obtained its raw material, wild mint, from the surrounding slopes of the valley. The mill was a short-lived venture as, like so many of the early wood-framed cotton mills, it burnt to the ground.

William Newton, a carpenter who had attracted the attentions of the Duke of Devonshire, had been working for the duke on The Crescent at Buxton. This was completed in 1785 and Arkwright then employed Newton to build the machinery for his mill at Cressbrook, the year it burnt down. Newton also dabbled in poetry and was nicknamed the 'Minstrel of the Peak' by the famous poetess of her day Anna Seward. The fire at Cressbrook destroyed everything Newton owned and it was only the financial assistance of his admirer Anna Seward which enabled him to survive until Barker Bossley bought the site from Arkwright. Bossley offered Newton a partnership and some time later Newton had amassed enough money to build the Cressbrook Mill that we see today. Newton had earned a reputation as a model

Former Cressbrook Mill

employer but this contrasts sharply with the evil character Ellis Needham at the nearby Litton Mill. According to
the albeit propagandist *Memoirs* of Robert Blincoe of
1832, who was an orphan boy and apprentice survivor
of the reign of Needham, the owner perpetrated some of
the very worst examples of nineteenth-century child
exploitation. There is very little other remaining evidence
today of what went on at the Litton Mill to support
Blincoe's claims, and whilst it is generally accepted that
the sufferings of the apprentices were undeniably terrible
it is thought that Blincoe may have exaggerated some of
the facts. Nonetheless these memoirs, which greatly
shocked many people, provided a well-overdue catalyst
for factory reform and improved conditions.

ROUTE INSTRUCTIONS

1 From the car park make your way to the front of
the Monsal Head Hotel. Standing with your
back to the hotel overlooking Monsal Dale there is
a cafe to the left. On the opposite side of the road
to the cafe is a public footpath sign. Turn right here
as signposted 'Access to Viaduct' and walk down

some steps. At a T-junction turn left by a public footpath sign for the 'Viaduct and Monsal Trail', still walking downhill through woodland to reach the trail. Turn right onto the trail and soon cross over the viaduct. Forty metres after the viaduct turn left and at the fork in front of you bear to the right uphill. Keep ahead at a T-junction so that you are now walking on a track. The track eventually levels out and the site of Fin Cop Hill Fort can be seen over to the left. This Iron Age fort, which by Peak District standards was quite large, is the only one found on limestone rather than gritstone. At a public footpath sign ignore the route to the left for Brushfield Hough and maintain direction through a number of gates to the hamlet of Brushfield.

2 At the far end of Brushfield turn left onto a lane. When the lane bends sharply to the left turn right by a public footpath sign into High Dale to walk by a wall on the right. When the wall ends at a crossroad of paths turn right to begin the ascent out of the dale. At the fork in 30m keep to the right on the main path to pass through a gap in the wall. At a fork in 40m bear to the left and negotiate another gap in the wall. Follow the right-hand edge of a wall and climb a stile onto a track.

3 Turn left onto the track and then in 40m turn right by a

View from Monsal Head

public footpath sign to follow the right-hand edge of a field. Climb a stile just to the left of a gate and turn right to walk by a wall through an old lead mining area. The path moves away from the wall and heads across the old workings and drops down to a stile. Climb the stile and walk downhill with a wire fence on the left through what is now a nature reserve littered with evidence of past lead mining activities. Climb a stile by the side of a gate and continue downhill on a grassy track to reach a railway bridge over the Monsal Trail.

4 Do not cross over the bridge but head down the steps to the right onto the trail. In 30m, following the Monsal Trail sign, the path bears to the left and heads down into woodland to cross a footbridge over the River Wye at Litton. Turn right after the bridge and walk between two large gateposts to pass Litton Mill. At the end of the mill the path bends to the right and then to the left to follow a delightful route through Miller's Dale and Water-cum-Jolly Dale. On crossing a footbridge at the end of the spectacular limestone gorge of Water-cum-Jolly bear to the left if you wish to visit a cafe

203

Weir on the Wye at Water-cum-Jolly

in 30m or if you would like a close-up view of Cressbrook Mill just past the cafe. More spectacular views of the mill and its complex will be reached by following the main route. Alternatively turn right and walk across a footbridge by a weir. The path bends to the right and then climbs round to the left to reach a level section of the Monsal Trail with Monsal Head in the distance. Follow the trail along the side of the Wye Valley and turn around for ever increasing views of Cressbrook Mill. Negotiate a gate and pass Monsal Railway Station to reach the Monsal Viaduct again. Cross over the viaduct and retrace your steps by turning left after the viaduct and head back uphill to a T-junction. Here turn right to return to Monsal Head.

Refreshments:	Hotel and cafe at Monsal Head and cafes close to both the Litton and Cressbrook mills
Toilets:	Car park at Monsal Head
Key Features:	The view of Monsal Dale and Monsal Viaduct from Monsal Head; the mills of Litton and Cressbrook; Miller's Dale and Water-cum-Jolly Dale; a section of the Monsal Trail

WALK 39
Peak Forest Canal and Torrs Riverside Park

Distance:	13km/8 miles
Start:	New Mills Leisure Centre on Hydebank Road
Map:	OS Explorer OL1 The Peak District Dark Peak Area
Terrain:	A varied walk on good quality paths with several moderate ascents

An Act of Parliament was passed in 1794 to build the Peak Forest Canal to provide an access route to transport limestone from Dove Holes. The canal terminated at the Bugsworth Basin and a 10.5km/6½ mile tramway was built up to the Dove Hole quarries, which stand 300m/985ft above sea level. The building of the canal was completed under the supervision of the engineer Benjamin Outram and the upper length was in use by

The Peak Forest Canal runs for 23km/14½ miles from the Ashton Canal at Ashton through Marple, New Mills and on to Whaley Bridge. In addition there is a branch arm to the Buxworth Basin (previously known as the Bugsworth Basin). The canal fell into disrepair in the 1950s but in more recent years has been restored to full navigation.

Peak Forest Canal

1800. It took 17 years from the opening of the canal for a dividend to be paid to the proprietors and it then continued in profit until the coming of the railways.

In 1825 a half mile/0.75km length was added to Whaley Bridge to provide a link with the Cromford and High Peak Railway to the Cromford Canal. Thus later in the canal's life it was used to transport goods other than limestone, such as coal, stone, cotton and grain. Then in 1846 the Sheffield, Ashton-under-Lyne and Manchester Railway Company leased the canal and later the Manchester, Sheffield and Lincolnshire Railway purchased it. Limestone trade through Bugsworth had ceased by 1922 and all regular trade on the canal dried up during the 1950s.

For information on New Mills and Torrs Riverside Park see Walk 40.

ROUTE INSTRUCTIONS

1 From the car park walk back to the entrance to the leisure centre and bear left down some steps to reach the Sett Valley Trail in a few metres. Turn right onto the trail. At a fork bear left into the

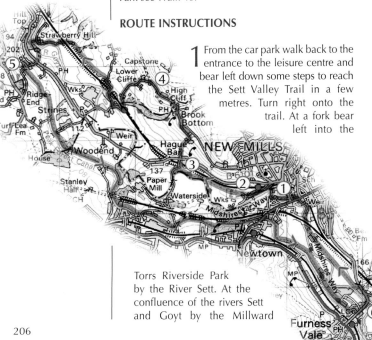

Torrs Riverside Park by the River Sett. At the confluence of the rivers Sett and Goyt by the Millward

Millennium Walkway, Torrs Riverside Park

Memorial Bridge turn right away from the bridge onto the Goyt Way. Pass under a bridge and at a fork keep right to reach the Millennium Walkway. Follow the walkway through the gorge and once at the other side ignore the footbridge on the left.

2 Keep to the clearly marked Goyt Way through the park to walk past an old gasworks on the right, which is now a garden. Shortly after the garden turn right to reach a gate next to an old barn in 20m. Immediately after the gate turn left as signposted for the Goyt Way through trees. Carefully follow the Goyt Way signs, keeping close to the river for a while before turning right away from it at a signpost to soon arrive at Hague Bar picnic site.

3 Turn right onto Waterside Road and cross over the B6101 onto a No Through Road called Hague Fold Road. The lane climbs uphill past Lower Hague Farm and bends to the left in front of Higher Hague Farm. At the end of the lane continue ahead along a rough track. The Cage in Lyme Park can be seen over to the left. Turn left on

reaching a lane, still on the Goyt Way, dropping down to the hamlet of Brook Bottom. Just before the Fox Inn turn left onto a bridleway along the Goyt Way.

4 Walk downhill to pass under a railway bridge and onto a cobbled lane. At the end of the cobbles turn right onto a bridleway signposted for Greenclough Farm. Follow an uphill track to the farm. Bear to the right in front of the farm and then turn left in 15m at a Goyt Way sign. At a fork keep to the right along the bridleway, to walk with a railway line on the left, and left at the next fork on the Goyt Way to pass Windy Bottom Farm. Shortly after the farm walk through a tunnel to reach the River Goyt. At Strawberry Hill Cottage turn left at a signpost for Strines to leave the Goyt Way and

Torrs Riverside Park

cross over an old packhorse bridge called Roman Bridge to walk upstream. Ignore the steps on the right in 20m and follow the track which moves away from the river and climbs up to a road. Cross over the road onto Plucksbridge Road. When the lane bends to the right bear left uphill to reach the Peak Forest Canal towpath in 30m.

5 Turn left onto the towpath and follow it for 5km/3 miles to Newtown near New Mills, where you will be met by the overwhelmingly sweet smell from the Swizzels sweet factory on the left. Pass under the A6015 and continue past New Mills Wharf. A mile/1½km further on at the far end of the long Furness Vale Marina leave the canal towpath at the bridge and turn left onto the road. Cross over the River Goyt and follow the road round to the left to reach Gowhole Farm.

6 Turn left at a public footpath sign just after Gowhole Farm. Pass through two gates to walk along a track with a wall on the left. Climb a stile at the side of a gate and follow a field edge with a signal box over to the right to another stile. For a short while you walk close to the River Goyt before walking between wire fences to pass Goytside Farm. Then walk under the 13-arch Midland Railway Viaduct. When the path forks bear left to keep by the river along the Goyt Way into the Torrs. Cross over Millward Memorial Bridge at the confluence of the rivers Sett and Goyt and turn right to retrace your steps to the starting point.

Refreshments:	Pubs, cafes and heritage centre at New Mills and the Fox Inn at Brook Bottom
Toilets:	Heritage centre at New Mills
Key Features:	Torrs Riverside Park; a section of the Goyt Valley Way; a section of the Peak Forest Canal

WALK 40
New Mills, Sett Valley Trail and Hayfield

The Sett Valley Trail runs for 4km/2½ miles from New Mills to Hayfield along the former Hayfield Railway Line built for the Midland and Great Central Joint Railway Company. New Mills is set amongst attractive but brooding hills on the edge of the Dark Peak, and it was the home of a thriving textile industry from the late eighteenth century to the 1960s. Hayfield was the starting point of the famous mass trespass of ramblers onto Kinder Scout in 1932 for the right to roam on forbidden moorland.

Distance:	12km/7½ miles
Start:	Torr Top car park (2 hour stay only), New Mills or Hayfield Station car park (Sett Valley Trail)
Map:	OS Explorer OL1 The Peak District Dark Peak Area
Terrain:	Flat trail walking to Hayfield with a climb on the return leg from Hayfield onto Ollersett Moor

Around 1390 a corn mill was built called New Mill. By the sixteenth century the name New Mill was a placename for a small settlement that had grown up around the mill. Later an industrial town began to develop on either side of the confluence of the rivers Sett and Goyt, and indeed the whole area between Hayfield, New Mills and Strines along the Sett and Goyt valleys became an important centre for the calico-printing industry. The plural form, New Mills, began to be used around 1775 and the parish of New Mills was created in 1884. This rapidly growing town concentrated on cotton spinning, bleaching and dying, and calico printing.

New Mills was particularly suited to the development of mills based on water power because of a dramatic natural gorge created during the Ice Age called the Torrs, which is a most unexpected and spectacular spot set 30m/100ft below the street level of the town. The ruined foundations of the mills and the weirs can be seen along the Torrs and the region has been turned into a country park, Torrs Riverside Park. This 'park under the town' contained until fairly recently a stretch of the ravine which was inaccessible to the public, however the building of the 160m/525ft Torrs Millennium

Walkway has transformed the park. The walkway is elevated high above the River Goyt and yet it sits deep within the gorge and is already proving very popular and drawing in visitors. The walkway is used in Walk 39.

Steam power began to be introduced into the mills in the 1840s and this sparked off a second phase of mill building in the vicinity alongside the Peak Forest Canal at New Town. A more detailed history of New Mills and its surroundings can be obtained from the excellent heritage and information centre 50m from the Torr Top car park.

The Sett Valley Trail was opened in 1868 and was kept busy for over 60 years by the textile mills and it also saw heavy passenger traffic. It was not unusual on summer Sundays in the 1920s for four to five thousand hillwalkers to arrive from Manchester at the station in Hayfield. The railway was closed in 1970 and was then purchased from British Rail by Derbyshire County Council in 1973 and was reopened as a recreational trail. The village of Hayfield sits at one end of the Sett Valley Trail at the confluence of the rivers Sett and Kinder. It is also at the crossroads of two former important moorland routes, first a packhorse track between Cheshire and Yorkshire and later a coach route from Glossop to Buxton. Like New Mills it has an industrial past in textiles.

ROUTE INSTRUCTIONS

1 From the car park the Torrs and Sett Valley Trail is signposted along a cobbled lane. In 20m turn left onto the Sett Valley Trail and keep left at the fork in front of you. Essentially the Sett Valley Trail signs are followed all the way to Hayfield Station across Church Lane, St George's Road, High Hill Road, Wildes Crossing and Station Road. The trail then passes Birch Vale Reservoir on the left with Lantern Pike set behind it and, after Slack's Crossing, Hayfield Station is soon reached.

2 Turn right onto the road and at a crossroads keep ahead on Chapel Street which leads onto

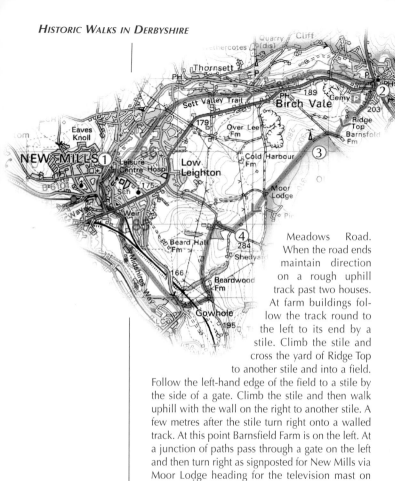

Meadows Road. When the road ends maintain direction on a rough uphill track past two houses. At farm buildings follow the track round to the left to its end by a stile. Climb the stile and cross the yard of Ridge Top to another stile and into a field. Follow the left-hand edge of the field to a stile by the side of a gate. Climb the stile and then walk uphill with the wall on the right to another stile. A few metres after the stile turn right onto a walled track. At this point Barnsfield Farm is on the left. At a junction of paths pass through a gate on the left and then turn right as signposted for New Mills via Moor Lodge heading for the television mast on Ollersett Moor.

3 Pass through a gate to the left of the mast and maintain direction along a thin but distinct path across the moor with New Mills in the distance. On reaching an airshaft which is marked by what looks like a trig point continue ahead,

making for the white building called Moor Lodge. The top of this building can be seen above a wall. Climb the ladder stile over this wall and follow a path to reach a lane by the lodge. Turn left onto the lane and in 30m opposite the lodge there are two public footpath signposts. Take the left-hand of these two paths and follow the right-hand edge of a number of fields to a derelict building. Pass to the right of this building to reach a lane.

4 Turn right onto Laneside Road. In 200m turn left onto a walled public bridleway which is opposite Brownhill Farm. In 30m at a fork bear to the left and follow the track past Howcroft Farm to reach a lane. Turn right onto the lane and pass under a railway bridge. The lane bends to the right to a T-junction. Turn right and then left at a public footpath sign just after Gowhole Farm. Pass through two gates to walk along a track with a wall on the left. Climb a stile at the side of a gate and follow a field edge with a signal box over to the right to another stile. For a short while you walk close to the River Goyt before walking between wire fences to pass Goytside Farm. Walk under the 13-arch Midland Railway Viaduct. When the path forks bear left to keep by the river along the Goyt Way into the Torrs. Cross over Millward Memorial Bridge at the confluence of the rivers Sett and Goyt and turn right. At a fork just before a bridge turn left up a cobbled lane and left again at the top to return to the starting point.

Refreshments:	Pubs, cafes and heritage and information centre in New Mills and Hayfield Station car park
Toilets:	New Mills Heritage and Information Centre and Hayfield Station car park
Key Features:	Sett Valley Trail; the Torrs; New Mills Heritage and Information Centre (01663 746904); Hayfield Information Centre at Hayfield Station

Distance:	5km/3 miles
Start:	Glossop town centre near the tourist information office
Map:	OS Explorer OL1 The Peak District Dark Peak Area
Terrain:	A short undulating walk with a 360-degree panorama of the surrounding moorland

Present-day Glossop, a 'Gateway to the Peak', sprawls across the valley floor cradled by the sombre moorland of Kinder, Bleaklow and Saddleworth. The Romans established a fort, Melandra Castle, to the northwest of the modern town of Glossop, just beyond the Gamesley Housing Estate, to guard the entrance to the Longdendale Valley Trans-Pennine route. All that remains of the fort and the surrounding settlement, dating from around AD 75, are the foundations. In Norman times William Peverel built a motte and bailey castle at Mouselow or Castle Hill. Bronze Age and Iron Age remains have also been found in the area of the castle.

Old Glossop, which lies east of the modern town, grew up at the junction of three turnpike routes on Glossop Brook, which then went on to cross the Pennines. It is a pretty mixture of seventeenth-century gritstone cottages and a church. The Duke of Norfolk largely rebuilt the church in 1853. Old Glossop may come as an unexpected surprise to those who frequently travel through Glossop to access the high and desolate Snake Pass route from Manchester to Sheffield, as its existence will no doubt have gone unnoticed.

It was the early nineteenth century which was to herald the greatest change for Glossop under the patronage of the Duke of Norfolk. At this time there were many mills, mainly producing cotton, strung out across Glossopdale. The duke built a planned industrial town of streets and Victorian cotton mills and he gave the town a fine range of public buildings including a market hall and a railway station. The mill town was built to the west of Old Glossop and was named Howardstown after the duke's family name. This was a time of prosperity for Glossop, which was to come to an abrupt end with the collapse of the cotton industry in the 1920s. Glossop was hit very severely indeed and it took a number of decades to recover.

ROUTE INSTRUCTIONS

1 At the crossroads of the A57 and the A624/B6105 turn right onto High Street East towards Sheffield. In 30m turn left onto Ellison Street and then in 50m turn right immediately after the Pentecostal Church. Maintain direction on a surfaced path through housing, and when the path appears to end on reaching King Edward Avenue turn right for 20m and then left to join a path next to a school. At the end of the school grounds there is a fork: keep ahead as the path drops down towards a lake. At another fork do not drop down to the lake but remain on the higher route, soon walking for a short distance between two walls, which leads to a road in Old Glossop.

2 In 100m bear to the right onto Church Walk. On reaching a road after passing the church turn right onto Church Street South and right again at a T-junction. After crossing Glossop Brook turn left in 20m onto Manor Park View. In 15m turn right onto a track with Hall Fold Farm on the left. After the cottages the track bends to the left. A hundred metres further on pass through a gap in the wall on the right into a field. Walk along the left-hand edge of the field for 50m and pass through another gap to follow a wire fence on the left. The path leads onto a playing field and you maintain direction along its left-hand edge. Just before reaching housing there is a narrow path off to the left which runs down the back of houses to meet a track. Turn left on reaching a road, which shortly arrives at the A57 with the Royal Oak on the left.

3 Cross over with care onto Hurst Road. The road passes the

entrance to Glossop and District Golf Club and starts to head uphill before bending to the left. Twenty metres before the entrance to Hurst Villa turn right but not onto the surfaced downhill track. Walk by a high wall on the left just after the surfaced track to a gate in 20m. Pass through a gap to the right of the gate and walk downhill with a wall on the right into housing. Maintain direction and cross over a road to reach the end of a cul de sac. Here bear to the left onto a path which leads to a road. Cross the road and turn right for a few metres before turning left over a brook. Walk with the housing on the left, ignoring any offshoots, to cross over another brook and reach a stile.

4 At the end of the housing 20m after the stile the path bends to the right to a junction. Turn left to walk uphill. The path bends to the right to provide good views over Glossop and its surroundings. Keep ahead at a T-junction of paths and 50m further on pass through a gap on the right into a field. Head across the middle of three small fields and follow the left-hand edge of the fourth field which bends to the left. At the end of the field turn right to walk downhill along its left-hand edge to reach a road. Turn left onto the road and at the junction in a few metres bear to the right to drop down to Glossop Brook. Do not cross over the brook but turn left onto a path to walk beside the brook. The path then swings left slightly away from the brook to reach a road. Turn right and then at the T-junction at the bottom of the hill turn right onto the A624 to return to the starting point.

Refreshments:	Pubs and cafes in Glossop and the Royal Oak on the A57 on the outskirts of Glossop
Toilets:	Glossop
Key Features:	Glossop

WALK 42
Three Shires Head and Flash

Distance:	6.5km/4 miles
Start:	Roadside parking by the church and school in the village of Flash just off the A53 several miles outside Buxton
Map:	OS Explorer OL24 The Peak District White Peak Area
Terrain:	Undulating moorland walk on high ground. Ensure good weather conditions before setting off. Potentially boggy ground on the climb up to Wolf Edge.

Three Shires Head is a remote but delightful spot marking the converging boundaries of Derbyshire, Staffordshire and Cheshire. It is also the meeting place of several former packhorse routes and streams by a fine gritstone packhorse bridge spanning the River Dove. These days the bridge provides a popular area for a picnic and paddling for children.

Flash is the highest village in England at 553m/1518ft and perhaps also the coldest, as winter starts early here and spring arrives late. The well-worn cottages are proof enough of the harsh weather conditions they have endured over the years. In the early nineteenth century the villagers were found to be counterfeiting coins to supplement the meagre living they were scraping from the land. The isolated position of the village, close to the border of three counties, made it ideal for concealing their illicit trade as at that time the police had no authority outside their own county. This discovery coined the phrase 'flash money', meaning counterfeit money.

ROUTE INSTRUCTIONS

1 Just after the church bear to the right at a junction to pass the New Inn on the left. You soon leave the cottages of Flash behind to descend on a very narrow lane. Pass Cross Side Cottage and then at the bottom of the hill, when the lane bends to the right, turn right onto a concrete driveway for

Far Brook Farm. Bear left in front of the farm to a gate and in 30m follow the path to the left of a gate.

2 On reaching a stile at the side of a gate climb over it and continue to reach a footbridge on the right by a footpath sign. Turn left here as signposted for Three Shires Head, initially scrambling up a bank to reach a stile by the side of a gate. Follow the right-hand edge of a field towards a farm. Do not pass the farm but climb a stile on the right just before it. Walk through the field to meet a track in 30m and turn right. In 50m turn left at a junction of paths as signposted for Three Shires Head.

3 After passing a cottage on the right keep to the right at a fork on a sandy track and disregard any paths off this track for several kilometres to reach the packhorse bridge at Three Shires Head. Do not cross over the bridge but instead turn right next to it to pass through a gate to climb uphill with a stream on the right. In several hundred metres turn right over a bridge and climb a stile immediately after it to join an uphill track. The track bends to the left at the top of the hill. On meeting a surfaced lane turn right. The lane bends to the right by Knotbury Farm, ignoring the public footpath straight ahead, and leads to a T-junction.

4 Turn left and in 150m look out for a marker post on the right and cross over a stone clapperbridge to begin the ascent over moorland to Wolf Edge. The path, which can be boggy up to the

Three Shires Head

edge, heads over to a broken-down wall in 50m which you cross over and turn right. Walk uphill with a wall on the right and keep ahead by a public footpath signpost to reach a stile. Climb the stile and turn left to negotiate another stile in 30m and soon reach the craggy outcrop of Wolf Edge.

5 Thirty metres to the right of the outcrop is a public footpath sign. Walk along a walled track for 75m and climb a stile at the side of a gate. Turn right to walk with a wire fence on the right. Climb a stile next to a gate and follow a walled track for 75m before climbing a stile into a field. Head across the middle of two fields and then make for a footpath sign just to the right of a cottage at Flash. Bear to the left and follow a track down to a lane. Turn left to return to the starting point.

Refreshments:	The New Inn at Flash
Toilets:	None
Key Features:	Three Shires Head and surrounding moorland, and the village of Flash

WALK 43
Birchen Edge

This walk passes two monuments erected to celebrate two British national heroes from the Napoleonic Wars: Vice-Admiral Horatio, Lord Nelson and the Duke of Wellington. Set back from Nelson's Monument on Birchen Edge are three boulders called the Three Ships. Individually they are named Victory, Defiance and Sovereign – all ships at the Battle of Trafalgar.

Distance:	7km/4½ miles
Start:	Birchen Edge car park on the B6050 just off the A619 near Robin Hood Inn between Baslow and Wadshelf
Map:	OS Explorer OL24 The Peak District White Peak Area
Terrain:	After a gradual climb onto Birchen Edge the next stretch across moorland can be slightly boggy. The remainder of the walk is across gently undulating ground.

Lord Nelson was a young and rising star in the Royal Navy, who was quickly rewarded for his inspiring leadership and military successes. In naval battles he lost an eye in 1794 and a right arm in 1797. Later in 1798 the French were destroyed at the key Battle of the Nile and in 1801 Nelson led another significant win against the Danes in the Battle of Copenhagen. During the French Wars from 1793 to 1802 Napoleon Bonaparte was winning victory after victory for France's citizen army and was elevated to Emperor of France. By 1805 he was making great plans for an invasion of England but it was Nelson who won the day at the memorable Battle of Trafalgar, at Cape Trafalgar off the Spanish coast, in which he died. Mourned by the whole nation Nelson received a state funeral in St Paul's Cathedral.

After Trafalgar Britain had another master tactician and strategist to follow Nelson. His name was Arthur Wellesley and as his military victories mounted he became a viscount, a marquis and finally Duke of Wellington. Wellington concentrated his efforts on the

Iberian Peninsula as he felt this presented the best opportunity to drain 'Boney's' armies and financial strength needed for conquests elsewhere. Slowly Wellington's plans proved effective and the Peninsular War was to be described by Napoleon as his 'Spanish ulcer'. Wellington, aided by General Blucher's Prussian army, was to prove once more to be a thorn in Napoleon's side, and Napoleon was finally defeated at the Battle of Waterloo in Belgium in 1815, although it was at an enormous cost of life. Wellington later went on to become prime minister and he even had a boot named after him.

According to legend at one time the young men of Baslow had to climb to the top of the Eagle Stone to prove their manhood to the local girls before they were allowed to marry.

ROUTE INSTRUCTIONS

1 Turn left out of the car park and then after a house bear to the left onto a track and pass through a gate in 20m. Climb some steps on the left to begin the gentle ascent through woodland onto Birchen Edge. At a fork keep ahead to eventually reach the bottom of the edge, which is popular with climbers. Nelson's gritstone monument can be seen on the top of the edge. Do not climb up onto the edge but continue ahead across moorland for several kilometres to reach a crossroads with the A621.

2 Cross over the road to follow the signpost for Curbar. In 150m turn left through a gate to walk along a track across moorland for several kilometres to reach Wellington's Monument. This

gritstone cross was erected in 1866. Over to the right the large boulder is known as the Eagle Stone. The path bends to the right by the monument. A hundred metres further on at a junction of paths bear to the left and maintain direction to reach a gate on the edge of the moorland.

3 Do not go through the gate but double back to the left along a grassy path to walk with a wall on the right, which later descends into woodland. At a fork bear to the right to descend to a stile to leave the moorland and a little further on to reach the A621. Cross over the road and climb the stile on the opposite side to the left of a house.

4 Follow the clear path through the woodland and maintain direction at a crossroads to climb gently uphill. Pass though a gap in a wall into a more open area surrounded by bracken before the path re-enters woodland. At the top of the hill pass through another gap in the wall. Shortly after there is a fork off to the left which you ignore to begin the descent to the A619. Turn left onto the road and bear left by the Robin Hood Inn onto the B6050 to return to the car park.

Refreshments:	Robin Hood Inn
Toilets:	None
Key Features:	Birchen Edge; Nelson's Monument; Wellington's Monument; the Eagle Stone

WALK 44
Pentrich

Distance:	5.5km/3½ miles
Start:	Roadside parking on Main Road, Pentrich, near St Matthew's Church
Map:	OS Explorer 269 Chesterfield & Alfreton
Terrain:	A gentle and easy stroll

In 1817 Pentrich was a thriving village in the process of change from an agricultural to an industrial village. The victory at Waterloo in 1815 began a period of severe economic depression. This created discontent across the country, but especially in the new industrial areas, which the government savagely repressed.

This encouraged groups to meet to seek political reform. Thomas Bacon, a Pentrich framework knitter, was very active in reform meetings in the North and Midlands. A revolt was being planned in 1817 in the Yorkshire/Nottingham area with the intention of marching to London to overthrow the government. Jeremiah Brandreth, a stockinger from Sutton in Ashfield, arrived in Pentrich on 5 June 1817 and took part in several meetings where it was agreed that the rising would be on 9 June and that they would meet at South Wingfield at 10pm and march first to Nottingham. Their march met with some resistance and resulted in the only death of the night when a man was shot. The men reassembled at Pentrich Lane End and marched on to the Butterley Ironworks, but their demands for arms and cannon shot were not met and they left empty handed for Nottingham. Demoralised, many of the men defected, but a small group made it across the Nottinghamshire border around dawn. The King's Hussars met them and the 'revolt' was quickly over.

The village of Pentrich in Derbyshire is closely linked with the story of England's last revolution in 1817. Until 1540 Pentrich belonged to Darley Abbey. Following the dissolution of the monasteries it passed to the Zouch family and then from 1634 to 1950 it was part of the Chatsworth Estate. Pentrich became very much involved in the Industrial Revolution as it is close to the Butterley Ironworks and the Cromford Canal (see Walk 34).

The three ringleaders, including Brandreth, were sentenced to be hanged, drawn and quartered; 14 men were transported to Australia and six were gaoled. The ringleaders in the end were granted 'clemency', and were hanged and beheaded. The houses of the guilty men were pulled down and their families lost their tenancies. The land was then redistributed to loyal tenants and from this time onwards Pentrich became smaller and gradually lost its importance to the expanding town of Ripley.

ROUTE INSTRUCTIONS

1 From the public footpath sign for Pentrich Mill next to the church climb the steps up into the churchyard. Just before the entrance to the church bear left onto a grassy path between gravestones. Pass through a gap into a field on the edge of the churchyard. Walk across the middle of the field towards a stile. Crich Stand can be seen half right in the distance. At nearly 364m/1000ft above sea level Crich Stand sits prominently on top of a limestone quarry ridge. This 23m/63ft beacon tower was erected in 1923 as a war memorial to the Sherwood Foresters in the First World War. At the fork of paths immediately after the stile keep ahead. Twenty metres past a field corner turn left through a gap and then right to follow the right-hand edge of a field. Climb a stile in the field corner and turn left to follow the left-hand edge of three fields to a junction of paths. Maintain direction through a gap to reach the B6013 opposite Pentrich Mill by the River Amber.

2 Cross over the B6013 and turn left. Keep ahead at Pentrich Lane End by the Devonshire Arms to reach the A610. Turn left and in 100m cross over the A610 with extreme care to a lane signposted for Lower Hartshay. Do not follow this lane but bear immediately to the right onto a track by a public footpath sign, which leads to Pear Tree Farm. Keep

ahead through the farm buildings onto an enclosed path. Climb a stile at the side of a gate but do not cross Starvehimvalley Bridge in front of you. Instead bear to the left onto the Cromford Canal and turn left away from the bridge. Climb a stile at the end of the water and follow the left-hand edge of the field to a hedge corner. At this point you leave the line of the canal and maintain direction crossing a footbridge over a stream and then another field to reach a lane.

3 Turn right onto the lane and then turn right again onto Bridle Lane opposite the George Inn into Lower Hartshay. Climb a stile by a public footpath sign on the left to rejoin the Cromford Canal. The canal itself becomes evident in 50m. Follow the towpath under a bridge after passing Bridge Farm on the other side of the canal and then walk up a steep flight of steps to reach the A610. Cross over the road with care and turn right for 20m. Then turn left and walk down a steep flight of steps to rejoin the canal. Maintain direction later, walking with a fence on the left to reach a lane. Cross over the lane and turn left to walk along the pavement. When the pavement ends cross over the road and ignore a T-junction to return to Pentrich.

Refreshments:	The Dog Inn at Pentrich, the Devonshire Arms at Pentrich Lane End and the George Inn at Lower Hartshay
Toilets:	None
Key Features:	The village of Pentrich and a section of the Cromford Canal

WALK 45
Elvaston Castle and Country Park

Distance:	5km/3 miles
Start:	Car park at Elvaston Country Park off the B5010 southeast of Derby. Brown tourism signs are provided from the A52 and A6.
Map:	OS Explorer 259 Derby
Terrain:	A gentle and easy stroll through parkland

Elvaston Castle Country Park provides a 'castle' built during the Gothic fervour of the early nineteenth century set in 240 acres of beautiful woodland and landscaped gardens packed with interest and variety. The property came into the possession of the Stanhope family, later Earls of Harrington, in 1539 and was retained by them until 1963. The Derby Corporation and Derbyshire County Council later jointly purchased the estate in 1969 and opened it as Britain's first country park. The park now regularly hosts large events on its showground such as the County Show and steam rallies.

The Stanhope family first came to Elvaston in the mid-sixteenth century when Henry VIII granted the manor of Elvaston to Michael Stanhope. His family became powerful landowners who by the mid-eighteenth century enjoyed the unusual status of holding three earldoms within one family. In 1742 William Stanhope was created First Earl of Harrington. It was the third earl who built the house we see today. Prior to that a brick-built manor house had been the family home for 200 years. A part of this is seen on the walk, as it is on the right-hand side of the south front and is clearly dated 1633.

The third earl commissioned in 1812 a leading architect of his day, James Wyatt, who became well known for his Gothic styles. Wyatt did not live to see his design work carried out but his plans were implemented under the supervision of Robert Walker from 1815 to 1819. The fourth earl completed the construction of the house. He commissioned another Gothicist devotee, Lewis Cottingham, to rebuild the east front and refurbish parts of the interior. Before becoming an earl, Viscount Petersham had earned a reputation as a leading Regency buck. This attracted the attention and the friendship of the Prince Regent who emulated his dandy clothes, his tea drinking and his addiction to snuff. 'Beau' Petersham's clothes were high fashion items and include

Elvaston Castle

the Petersham overcoat and the Harrington hat. Petersham became embroiled in a much talked about affair with a London actress, Marie Foote, 17 years his junior, to the displeasure of his father and the delight of the society groups. After his father's death he married Marie in 1831 and they moved to Elvaston Castle where they led a secluded life for the next 20 years until the earl's death.

The estate was at this time still not landscaped and the fourth earl employed William Barron to undertake this work. Barron created a winter garden which by the 1840s had become a showcase for rare and interesting plants. Elvaston elevated Barron to a prominent figure in the horticultural world and he became a leading authority in coniferae. In an 1899 edition of *Country Life* it was said of Elvaston 'among the many regal gardens of England few are more remarkable'.

The fifth earl opened the estate to the public and despite the high entrance fee of 3 shillings the crowds flocked to view the gardens. In the late 1930s the eleventh earl left Elvaston for Ireland where the family still live. During the Second World War the property was used as a teacher training college but in 1963 the eleventh earl decided to sell the estate to a development company to meet the expense of death duties. In 1969 Derby Corporation and Derbyshire County Council made a joint purchase for the establishment of a country park. The park was opened a year later and an extensive programme of restoration of the gardens began. More than twenty years later the grounds are well established again and a wide range of facilities are available to the public.

ROUTE INSTRUCTIONS

1 From the car park walk back towards the B5010 and just before the entrance turn left onto a broad track. Follow this track, disregarding any off-shoots close to the edge of the park with the show-ground on the left, eventually crossing a bridge over the lake to reach a T-junction. The castle and St Bartholomew's Church are over to the left. Turn right and pass a sign for the Estate Museum on the left in 20m. This museum tells the story of country life at the beginning of the twentieth century. Join a plankway and at a junction of paths turn right to walk past the riding centre on the left.

2 Immediately after the riding centre turn left at a footpath sign for Elvaston and then turn left at the next T-junction. Continue ahead on reaching a sur-faced lane to reach the elaborate blue and gold cast iron gate. The

Golden Gates, a symbol of Elvaston, mark the southern end of the formal gardens. The Third Earl of Harrington brought them from the Palace of Versailles and erected them in 1819. There is an unverified story that they were originally at the royal palace in Madrid until Napoleon looted them. Turn left through the gates into the formal garden and when the track bends to the right maintain direction to pass through the Moor's Arch, which was the topiary handiwork of Barron. Cross over the parterre garden to reach the south front of the castle. Turn left in front of the castle and soon pass through an archway into the castle courtyard.

3 Bear half right across the courtyard to walk under another archway and immediately turn left onto a path walking towards the lake. On reaching the lake turn left to walk beside the edge of the lake. To begin with there is no path on the ground but you soon pass through a gate which leads to a T-junction. Turn right to cross the bridge in the opposite direction to that walked earlier. Immediately after the bridge turn right and follow the lakeside path past Barron's numerous artificial rock formations. After a small children's playground on the left cross over a bridge and then bear to the left over another bridge to return to the car park.

Refreshments:	Tea room in the courtyard
Toilets:	By the entrance to the country park
Key Features:	Elvaston Castle Country Park and the Estate Museum (01332 573799)

WALK 46
Melbourne Hall

Distance:	9km/5½ miles
Start:	Melbourne Hall, Melbourne
Map:	OS Explorer 245 The National Forest
Terrain:	A gentle walk through fields and along tracks on mainly level terrain

Melbourne Hall is in a lovely setting overlooking the mill pool on the edge of the small town of Melbourne. It is the family home of Lord and Lady Ralph Kerr, who is a direct descendant of Sir John Coke, a secretary of state for Charles I, who purchased the estate in 1629. The hall has therefore remained in the hands of the same family, including two Victorian prime ministers, for nearly 400 years, although the family name has changed several times due to inheritances via the female line.

Melbourne Hall lies on the site of a palace used by the Bishops of Carlisle until the fourteenth century. Melbourne Castle was demolished in the seventeenth century, leaving Melbourne Hall as the most important house in the parish. Sir Thomas Coke, grandson of Sir John Coke, made most of the alterations to the hall and he extended and greatly changed the gardens. The gardens today are now considered amongst the most notable in the country and include the famous yew tunnel and an elaborate wrought-iron domed cage known as the 'birdcage', made by Robert Bakewell around 1710. By marriage the hall passed from the Cokes to the Lambs and when Peniston Lamb was created a peer in 1770 he chose to adopt the title Lord Melbourne. His son William

Melbourne Hall Church from millpond

Lamb, the Second Lord Melbourne, was to become prime minister of the country and gave his name to the city of Melbourne in Australia. When William died the estate passed to his sister who remarried Lord Palmerston – the second prime minister from Melbourne Hall.

ROUTE INSTRUCTIONS

1 Walk to the left of the Church of St Michael and St Mary and pass through a gateway to reach the mill pool. Follow the surfaced path around the pool passing Melbourne Hall on the left. At the end of the pool ignore the first public footpath sign on the right and continue on to the next signpost in 30m. Pass through a gate into a field. Follow the path across a field to a stile and then walk through a field towards woodland. In the third field the path moves over to the left-hand edge of the field by trees.

2 When you are opposite a farm drop down some steps in the field corner to climb a stile. Keep to the left-hand edge of the field and maintain direction in the next field on a track. At a public footpath sign continue ahead along the right-hand edge of a field and just before the end of this field bear to the right off the track to a stile. Walk along the right-hand side of the field with woodland on the right. When the track bends to the right into the woodland keep ahead to a gate. At the end of the woodland continue across the middle of a field to a stile next to a large sign advising that you are now on a permissive path provided by the Staunton Harold Estate. Turn right after the stile to follow the field edge to a marker post. Bear right at the marker post to cross over a footbridge and walk along the left-hand edge of a field to reach the B587.

3 Turn left onto the B587 and then turn left at a T-junction in 200m just past Springwood Farm.

The lane bends to the left by Scotlands Farm and then back to the right. Ignore the first signpost on the left and carry on to the second in 100m when the lane bends sharply to the right to join a bridleway.

4 Follow the left-hand edge of a field as it soon bends to the right and then to the left. The church on the top of Breedon Hill comes into view on the right. Keep ahead at a marker post and when the track bends to the right maintain direction as indicated by a marker post to walk along the right-hand edge of a field. The path soon bends to the right and immediately to the left so that you are following the left-hand edge of fields again. Opposite Park Farm the track becomes a surfaced lane with a golf course on the right.

5 A hundred and fifty metres along the surfaced lane turn left at a public footpath sign to walk across the middle of a field towards two properties. On meeting a track climb a stile at the other side. Head diagonally across a field to a stile and continue in the same direction to another stile. Cross a cattle grid 20m after the stile and bear right off the track to head diagonally through a field. Walk through several fields via stiles to reach a road. Turn left onto the road into Melbourne and return to the starting point.

Refreshments:	Melbourne Hall Craft Centre
Toilets:	Melbourne Hall Craft Centre
Key Features:	Melbourne Hall (craft centre open most days of the year, gardens April to September and the hall in August – 01332 862502)

WALK 47
Errwood Hall and Goyt Valley

Distance:	9km/5½ miles
Start:	Errwood Hall car park, although it will be necessary to start the walk from the Pym Chair car park on Sundays or bank holidays
Map:	OS Explorer OL24 The Peak District White Peak Area
Terrain:	A moorland walk which although not difficult should be saved for fine weather conditions. The stretch from Pym Chair to Shining Tor can become a little boggy.

The Upper Goyt Valley is a seemingly endless expanse of wild rolling moorland which was partially tamed in the nineteenth century by the activities of the Grimshawe family who built Errwood Hall. In essence the Goyt Valley is the Dark Peak in microcosm and much of it is a designated Site of Special Scientific Interest.

The River Goyt once marked the boundary between the Royal Forest of the Peak to the east and Macclesfield Forest to the west. Later Stockport Corporation dammed the river to build first Fernilee Reservoir in 1938 and then Errwood Reservoir in 1967, holding 1087 and 927

Errwood Reservoir

million gallons respectively. Errwood is also the home of a popular sailing club. The Forestry Commission added to the man-made landscape by planting blocks of conifers in 1963 and the valley became the subject of a pioneering traffic management scheme in the early 1970s.

By 1830 the Grimshawes, a devout Roman Catholic family, owned much of the Upper Goyt Valley, having prospered from the Lancashire textile industry. Samuel Grimshawe constructed Errwood Hall in 1840 as a wedding present for his son. It was a palatial Italian-style residence surrounded by 40,000 rhododendron and aza-lea bushes brought back to England after many foreign trips on the family's yacht *Mariquita*. The flowers are ablaze in May/June. The Grimshawes built the Spanish Shrine in 1889, a small gritstone building constructed in Mediterranean style in memory of the family gov-erness from Spain, and there are always fresh flowers inside the tiny chapel. Errwood Hall was demolished partly in the interests of water purity when Fernilee Reservoir was built, leaving only a few ruins.

ROUTE INSTRUCTIONS

1 Standing with your back to the reservoir follow the Woodland Walk sign next to an information board about the Goyt Valley. At the fork in 20m bear to the right and pass through a gap in the wall into the gardens of Errwood Hall. At a T-junction turn right to walk through the delightful valley to a marker post for Errwood Hall. Here turn right to soon pass the ruins of the hall and continue on to

the end of the woodland where you cross some stepping-stones over a stream. A few metres further on at a junction of paths ignore the footbridge on the left and turn right to climb some steps. In 10m turn left at a public footpath sign for the Shrine and Pym Chair. Follow the clearly defined path for several kilometres along Foxlow Edge, passing the Spanish Shrine several hundred metres before reaching a lane known as The Street.

2 Turn left onto The Street and follow it uphill to Pym Chair. At the top of the hill turn left at the public footpath for Shining Tor. The car park, if starting from Pym Chair, is just beyond the top of the hill so you would turn left out of the car park and right at the top of the hill for Shining Tor. Follow the ridge top by a wall on the right for 5km/3 miles to reach a wall corner close to a ladder stile. The trig point for Shining Tor is just on the other side of the ladder stile.

3 Do not climb the stile but follow the path around to the left, dropping downhill and then climbing back up to a stile. After the stile turn left to walk by a wall on the left. At a public footpath signpost follow the direction indicator along a grassy path for Errwood Hall car park, dropping down towards the reservoir and immediately moving away from the wall. Pass through a gate and continue downhill to reach a crossroad of paths. Keep ahead between two gateposts to reach the car park.

Refreshments:	None
Toilets:	None
Key Features:	Goyt Valley and the gardens and ruins of Errwood Hall

WALK 48
Osmaston

Osmaston is an idyllic mellow red-brick estate village to the now demolished Osmaston Manor. Some of the cottages are thatched, which is fairly unusual for Derbyshire.

Distance:	7km/4½ miles
Start:	Roadside parking by the church at Osmaston. Osmaston is approached from the A52 near Ashbourne
Map:	OS Explorer 259 Derby
Terrain:	A flat walk, although on the return leg the woodland section can be a little boggy

The only remains of Osmaston Manor is a tower which can be seen on this walk, standing above the trees in Osmaston Park. The manor house was built in 1849 for Francis Wright and was pulled down in 1964 when the owner, Sir Ian Walker, moved to Okeover Hall near Ashbourne.

Waterwheel, Osmaston

ROUTE INSTRUCTIONS

1 From the church walk along the road into the village passing the Shoulder of Mutton pub. Turn left by the village pond and when the lane bends to the right continue ahead along the bridleway to Shirley. This clear track passes through two plantations and then drops down to pass between two lakes. There is a waterwheel on the lake. The track climbs back up and out of the woodland and then follows the edge of the woods. On meeting the surfaced Park Lane maintain direction, passing Shirley House and Park Lane Farm to reach a T-junction. It is recommended that you turn right here to explore the village of Shirley and its interesting pub before returning to this point.

2 By the T-junction, which you approach from Osmaston, there is a public footpath sign on the right by some steps. Climb a stile and follow the left-hand edge of a field

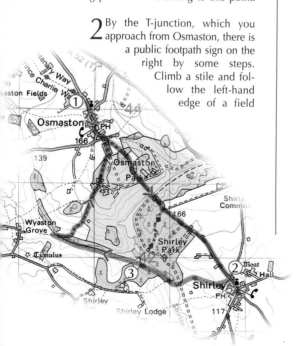

which bends to the right to reach a stile in the far corner. Climb the stile and turn right to reach another stile. Head across the field with views of Park Lane Farm over to the right to a stile. After the stile turn left and walk to another stile. Maintain direction to cross a footbridge in 75m. Turn right after the footbridge to follow a path into woodland to a junction of paths. Turn right over a second footbridge and continue past a marker post. Keep ahead on meeting a track and when this track bends to the left maintain direction to a gate on the edge of the woodland.

3 Continue on, passing a lake on the right to climb three stiles before Wyaston Grove comes into view. At a T-junction turn right and pass through a gate in 30m. Cross over Wyaston Brook and emerge from the trees in 100m onto a track which climbs gently uphill passing a plantation on the left. Climb a stile at the top of the hill and continue along the track with the tower of the demolished Osmaston Manor rising above the trees to reach a surfaced lane. At a fork on the lane bear to the left by a corrugated building and follow the lane round to the right. After the cricket pitch turn left at a T-junction to follow a driveway back to the village pond in Osmaston, where you retrace your steps to the church.

Refreshments:	Pubs at Osmaston and Shirley
Toilets:	None
Key Features:	The villages of Osmaston and Shirley, and Osmaston Park

WALK 49
Hathersage and River Derwent

Distance:	11.5km/7 miles
Start:	Car park on Oddfellows Road off the B6001 in Hathersage
Map:	OS Explorer OL1 The Peak District Dark Peak Area
Terrain:	The first half of the walk is on level ground mainly beside the River Derwent. The second half follows an undulating route.

During the eighteenth century millstones, which were quarried from the nearby gritstone edges, were the main trade of the village of Hathersage. Then in the nineteenth century it became a centre for the manufacture of pins and needles using five mills. The life of the mills was, however, fairly short, along with the lives of the men who were involved in the grinding of the points, who inhaled the resultant lethal dust.

Hathersage has two main claims to fame. The first is that the alleged grave of 'Little John', the companion and right-hand man of Robin Hood, is in the churchyard near the south door. The true identity of this elusive outlaw and man of the people has never been established but the legend and the enigma live strongly on. It is said that the grave was opened in the late eighteenth century and that a 32 inch/90cm thigh bone was found that would suggest a man about 7ft/2m tall. Despite the lack of

Hathersage is an attractive village which stands at the eastern entrance to the Hope Valley in excellent countryside above the River Derwent and beneath the gritstone edges. In recent years Hathersage has enlarged considerably as commuters from Sheffield have flocked into the area, and it is difficult to imagine that in the nineteenth century it was a dirty, smoky village.

Little John's head-stone, Hathersage churchyard

239

Hathersage and its church

evidence the grave brings life to the tales and acts as a tourist magnet to the area.

Hathersage also has strong connections with Charlotte Brontë's *Jane Eyre*, published in 1847. Charlotte stayed at Hathersage Vicarage for three weeks in 1845 and many associations with the region can be identified in the novel. For example, Hathersage was Morton after the landlord of the George Hotel, and Eyre was the name of the local lord of the manor. It is claimed that the patriarch of the Eyre family, Robert Eyre from Highlow Hall, built a hall for each of his seven sons within sight of his own hall. One of these, North Lees Hall, can be identified as Thornfield Hall in *Jane Eyre*. This building is a three-storied Tudor tower house, a style usually only seen further north. The National Park Authority now owns the North Lees Estate.

The Church of St Michael, which is mainly fourteenth century, stands prominently above the village and contains numerous fine memorial brasses to the powerful local Eyre family.

ROUTE INSTRUCTIONS

1 Turn right out of the car park and then turn left onto the B6001. Just before a railway bridge turn right onto Dore Lane and pass under another railway bridge. When the lane bends to the right climb a stile on the left to join a broad track. After

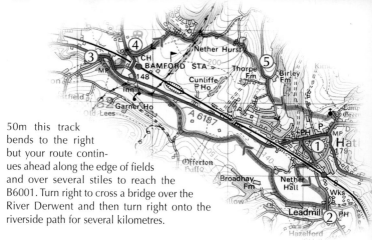

50m this track bends to the right but your route continues ahead along the edge of fields and over several stiles to reach the B6001. Turn right to cross a bridge over the River Derwent and then turn right onto the riverside path for several kilometres.

2 Along the riverside you cross two footbridges in quick succession and later pass some stepping-stones when you are virtually opposite Offerton Hall which is set on the hillside over to the left. You then cross another footbridge over a stream running down into the river and walk past Kentney Barn. After crossing another two footbridges you reach a lane.

3 Turn right to cross the River Derwent and then turn right onto the A625, passing the High Peak Garden Centre on the left. In 50m cross over the river again by using a footbridge and then turn immediate left after the bridge. In 75m when the river bends to the left there is a stile set behind a hedge which leads into a field. Follow the left-hand edge of the field and pass under a railway bridge into a caravan/camping area. Keep ahead for 30m and then turn left onto the driveway for the site. Turn right onto a road and then left at a T-junction in 40m onto Saltergate Lane.

4 Walk up the lane with Sickleholme golf course on the right. At a T-junction turn right onto Hurstclough Lane, which soon becomes a rough track and drops downhill before climbing back up

again. At the top of the hill pass through a gate on the right by a public bridleway sign. At Nether Hurst when the track bends to the right climb a stile in front of you to continue along the bridleway. Walk downhill along the right-hand edge of a field to cross a spring and then climb back uphill passing a metal gate and then climbing some steps to reach another gate. Follow the left-hand edge of a field by a line of trees which leads to a gate out onto a lane.

5 Turn right onto the lane with magnificent views of Stanage Edge over to the left. At a T-junction maintain direction towards Hathersage along Coggers Lane. Climb a stile into a field by a public footpath sign on the left. Walk half right across the field and maintain direction in the next field to a stile in the far left-hand corner. Climb the stile and then climb another stile immediately on the left. Walk steeply downhill to cross a surfaced lane and continue on for 50m to a footbridge over Hood Brook. Pass through a squeeze stile and follow a path which heads across a field away from the river to a gate. Turn right onto a track and then in 30m climb a stile on the left. Walk half left across the field to a gate into the churchyard. Walk through the churchyard, visiting Little John's grave to the right of the south door, and then turn right on reaching a road. Drop downhill and continue ahead at a junction to pass the Scotsman's Pack on the left. At a T-junction turn right to walk along the main road through Hathersage. There are toilets on the right-hand side of the road. Opposite the George Hotel turn left onto the B6001 and then left again to the car park as signposted.

Refreshments:	Pubs and cafes in Hathersage and a cafe at High Peak Garden Centre
Toilets:	Hathersage
Key Features:	The village of Hathersage and a section of the River Derwent

WALK 50
Hathersage and Stanage Edge

Distance:	11.5km/7 miles
Start:	Car park on Oddfellows Road off the B6001 in Hathersage
Map:	OS Explorer OL1 The Peak District Dark Peak Area
Terrain:	There is a long gradual climb up onto Stanage Edge at the start. Take care along the rocks of Stanage Edge and on the descent when leaving the edge. A gentle downhill walk back to Hathersage. Only attempt in fine, still weather conditions.

For information on Hathersage see Walk 49.

1 Turn right out of the car park and right at the T-junction onto the B6001. Then at the next T-junction turn right again onto the A625, and after passing the Hathersage Inn on the left turn left onto School Lane. Pass the Scotsman's Pack on the right and follow the road round to the right as it starts to climb uphill along The Dale eventually

Stanage Edge

leaving the cottages and renovated mill buildings of Hathersage behind. After 1.5km/1 mile the road bends sharply to the left. On the bend there is a public footpath to the right, which you ignore. Twenty metres further on bear to the right onto a track. The track drops downhill and crosses a stream before climbing back uphill much more steeply. The track becomes a path as you climb uphill to the summit and then maintain direction to meet a road with views of Higger Tor and Carl Wark on the right. Turn left onto the road and keep ahead at the T-junction. The road bends first to the left and then when it bends to the right bear to the left onto a path. Burbage Brook Valley is over to the right.

2 The path heads across moorland before climbing up onto Stanage Edge. Turn left, having climbed onto the edge, to shortly reach a trig point. Continue along the edge for 3km/2 miles using the road junctions at the bottom of the edge as guide points, along with Stanage Pole which can be seen in the distance over to the right. Below the edge the area is littered with abandoned millstones. Having passed an area of woodland on the left you can see a path climbing up to the edge. Just after passing a marker post and a junction of paths you bear to the left onto the path which you could see running up to the edge. This slabbed path drops down to gate. Pass through the gate to enter woodland. At the far side of the wood pass through another gate. There is a car park and an

alternative starting point over to the right, otherwise you head for a toilet block by the side of the road.

North Lees Hall

3 Climb the stile to the left of the toilet block and head downhill. Turn right at a T-junction and walk through a conifer plantation to a stile at the side of a gate. At the fork of paths immediately after the stile keep ahead towards North Lees Hall along a grassy path to a gate. Just after the gate at a junction of paths turn sharp left to skirt around North Lees Hall and join a surfaced driveway which drops down to a lane. Turn right onto the lane and pass Bronte Cottage on the right. When the lane bends to the left 20m after the cottage turn left by a public footpath sign to follow the left-hand edge of a field. The path bears slightly to the left, passing Brookfield Manor on the right. Follow the gravel path with a wire fence on the left to a stile. Head across the middle of a field and at a T-junction in the middle of the field turn right onto a track to reach a stile at the side of gate. Maintain direction across several fields and then bear to the right in front of a house to join a track. The track passes houses and a cricket ground to reach the A625. Turn right and then left back onto the B6001 and left again to return to the car park.

Refreshments:	Pubs and cafes in Hathersage
Toilets:	Hathersage
Key Features:	The village of Hathersage and Stanage Edge

WALK 51
Holloway and Dethick

Distance:	7km/4½ miles
Start:	High Peak Junction car park near Lea Bridge
Map:	OS Explorer OL24 The Peak District White Peak Area
Terrain:	An up and down walk which is moderately demanding

Florence Nightingale, the Lady of the Lamp, whose shadow the sick soldiers of the Crimean War kissed as she passed through their wards at night, became a national heroine. Until this time she had spent much of her life at the family home, Lea Hurst, near the hamlet of Holloway. Dethick was the birthplace of Anthony Babington, ringleader of the famous Babington Plot to assassinate Queen Elizabeth I, replace her with Mary Stuart (Mary Queen of Scots) and foster the Catholic movement.

Florence Nightingale was born in Florence, Italy, in 1820 whilst her wealthy parents were travelling around Europe. Her father, William Shore, changed his name to Nightingale when he inherited a large estate from his uncle Peter Nightingale II. It was the industry in a valley neighbouring Cromford, together with lead mining and property such as Lea Hall, which was the source of the Nightingale prosperity. In 1821 the family returned from their foreign travels and came to Lea in Derbyshire. Here they built Lea Hurst, but soon found it too cold, small and isolated from the London social scene. Lea Hurst therefore quickly became their summer residence and they purchased a further home at Embley Park, Hampshire.

From an early age Florence developed an interest in caring for people, and totally against her parents' wishes she trained as a nurse. At this time nursing was considered a much despised branch of domestic service which only the very poor would take up as an occupation. Despite continuing opposition from her family, in 1853 she was appointed to manage London's Institution for the Care of Sick Gentlewomen in Distressed Circumstances. A year later the Crimean War broke out and Florence took 38 nurses to Scutari and dramatically reduced the death rate of injured soldiers, which transformed her into a national figure.

Less than two years later she returned to England and worked tirelessly to improve hospital conditions and reform public health. In 1860 she founded the first Training School for Nurses at St Thomas's Hospital in London and provided the catalyst to elevate nursing to a respectable middle-class profession. After the Crimean War Florence spent most of her time in London, as the centre of political power, but she continued to visit Lea Hurst until 1880, when both her parents had died. In 1907 she became the first woman to be invested with the Order of Merit a few years before her death in 1910.

Lea Gardens are open daily from late March to the end of June and contain a nationally recognised and unique collection of rhododendrons and azaleas that have been introduced from all over the world.

Peter Nightingale, a lead merchant and smelter, set up a **mill at Lea Bridge** in 1784 powered by Lea Brook which flowed into the River Derwent. Nightingale's mill was later sold to a hosier, Thomas Smedley. His son John Smedley built Riber Castle and he founded the first great hydropathic establishment at Matlock. The mill was converted to produce wool and still survives, surrounded by a complex which has grown around it.

ROUTE INSTRUCTIONS

1 Return to the car park entrance and turn right onto the lane. At the junction in Lea Bridge turn left onto Lea Road, passing through the John Smedley Mill complex which straddles Lea Road. Pass a housing area on the right and then an isolated cottage. A hundred metres further on turn right onto a walled path just before woodland on the left to reach a lane.

2 Cross over the lane and turn left for a few metres before turning right at a public footpath sign by the Old Chapel House. The path runs between rhododendrons to reach a lane. Turn right onto the lane and pass the entrance to Lea Gardens. Just after the entrance to Lea Gardens a public footpath crosses the lane. Turn left onto an enclosed path with playing fields over to the left. At a T-junction turn left onto

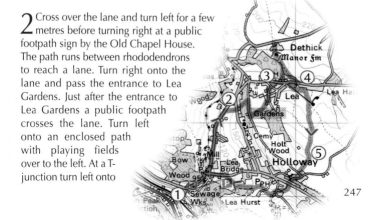

a track and on reaching a rough lane bear to the left through Lea. Cross over Holt Lane to a public footpath across a play area to reach a lane. The route turns right but there is a pub to the left.

3 Turn left in 20m at a public footpath sign for Dethick and Tansley. Cross over a footbridge straddling a brook and walk through Swinepark Wood. Climb a stile at the edge of the wood and walk along the left-hand edge of a field with the woodland still on the left. Climb a stile and head towards the church at Dethick. This church dates back to the thirteenth century and was the private chapel of Dethick manor, which was enlarged in 1530 by the Babington family. After exploring the hamlet of Dethick retrace your steps to the church and head back across the field towards Swinepark Wood. After climbing the stile you crossed earlier there is a fork in 20m. Bear to the left across the field to a stile at the edge of woodland. The path drops down and crosses a footbridge to reach a lane in Lea.

4 Turn right onto the lane and 30m after Lea Chapel double back left on yourself onto a track signposted for Upper Holloway and Wakebridge. At the end of the track climb a stile into a field. Walk diagonally across the field to the far left-hand corner and pass through a gap and then through another gap opposite. Head half left across the field and drop down onto a sunken path. At the signpost in 20m keep ahead as directed to Upper Holloway. The sunken path later emerges onto a track. When this track bends to the right climb a stile on the left into a field. Pass a field corner in 20m and maintain direction to a stile at the side of a gate. Head across the middle of the next field to a stile. Crich Stand sits prominently on Crich Cliff over to the left. This beacon tower was erected in 1923 as a war memorial to

the Sherwood Foresters in the First World War. Walk across the middle of another field to a stile at the side of gate and follow the left-hand edge of a field towards Upper Holloway Farm to reach a lane.

5 Turn left onto Long Lane and then right at the T-junction onto Upper Holloway. In 30m pass through a gap in the wall on the left and at a fork in 10m turn right, dropping steeply down steps to reach a lane. Cross over to a white gate by a public footpath sign and continue downhill. The path bends to the right and joins a surfaced lane. At a T-junction turn left and just after Bracken Cottage turn right by a public footpath sign onto an enclosed path. At a path junction keep ahead along the left-hand edge of a field to reach the driveway to Lea Hurst, once the home of Florence Nightingale and her parents. Maintain direction along the left-hand edge of the next field and then follow a high wall around to the left to a stile. Climb the stile and walk next to a high wire fence to another stile. Follow the right-hand edge of the next field to reach a gate providing access onto a lane. Turn left and follow the lane back to Lea Bridge and around to the left back to the starting point.

Refreshments:	Pub at Lea. Cafe at High Peak Junction – this is not on the route of the walk but is signposted over the River Derwent and Cromford Canal from the car park at the starting point.
Toilets:	None unless visiting the information point/cafe at High Peak Junction described above
Key Features:	John Smedley's Mill and factory shop (01629 534571); Dethick, once the home of the Babington family; the Lea/Holloway area associated with Florence Nightingale; Lea Gardens (01629 534380)

WALK 52
Midland Railway Centre and Codnor Castle

Distance:	9.5km/6 miles
Start:	Car parks at either end of Codnor Park Reservoir on the Cromford Canal near Ironville, or the car park in the Market Place at Codnor opposite the Red Admiral pub
Map:	OS Explorer 269 Chesterfield & Alfreton
Terrain:	A flat walk which presents no particular difficulties

The Midland Railway was created in the middle of the nineteenth century and became one of Britain's most important railways. The Midland Railway Centre, set in a 35 acre country park, includes a huge railway museum with a collection of steam and diesel locomotives and a 5.5km/3½ mile heritage railway.

The Lords Grey of Codnor built Codnor Castle in the twelfth century, although a castle had stood on the site from Norman times. When the estate was sold by the Zouch family in 1634 the castle fell into decay, and all that now remains is ruins.

The Midland Railway Centre commemorates a major railway company of its time and is operated by the Midland Railway Trust. The original Butterley station was demolished, and the building you see today was moved stone by stone from Whitwell in North Derbyshire. The heritage Golden Valley Light Railway is laid largely on the trackbed of the former Butterley Company railway. This linked its Butterley and Codnor Park Works to transport coal and ironstone from pits in the Butterley Park and Golden Valley areas.

The Butterley Ironworks dominated the expansion of this area during the Industrial Revolution. In 1790 Benjamin Outram and Francis Beresford established a company to mine coal and ironstone on the Butterley Hall Estate and they built an ironworks on the line of the Cromford Canal (see Walk 34). William Jessop, the canal's chief engineer, joined the project. The various ironworks and a number of local limestone quarries, collieries and mineral deposits prospered enormously from the Napoleonic Wars and then later under the ownership of William Jessop Jr. By 1839 Butterley was the largest owner of coal in the East Midlands area and the second largest producer of iron, and continued as a major contributor to the local economy well into the twentieth century. Jessop's Monument, a 25m/70ft high stone tower built in 1854 to commemorate the work of William Jessop Jr, can be seen at various points along this walk.

ROUTE INSTRUCTIONS

1 With your back to the reservoir turn right and cross over a footbridge at the end of the reservoir. At a junction after the footbridge bear to the left to follow the canal towpath to reach a road. Newlands Inn is on the opposite side of the road. Walk around either side of the barrier on the other side of the road and take the footpath at the back of the pub to continue along the canal towpath into the Midland Railway Centre Country Park. This path is open at the discretion of the Midland Railway Trust.

2 Watch out for steps on the right to take a path which doubles back through woodland to reach the Newlands Inn end of the Golden Valley Light Railway. Climb a stile by the railway track and turn left to climb another stile in a few metres. Follow the path through woodland and at a fork bear to the left and soon cross over a wooden bridge. At a fork immediately after the bridge bear to the left to walk along the edge of the woodland. Keep ahead at a railway bridge on the right, and at a junction of paths in a more open area bear to the left to cross a wooden bridge over a stream. At a fork just after the bridge bear to the right and climb up to the Golden Valley Light Railway. This next stretch follows the railway line until you reach a gate which enables you to cross over the track. At this point you can see the Victorian Railwayman's church.

3 At the fork in front of you bear to the left to walk uphill with trees on the left to pass the

Western Up Cast. This was used as an airshaft and emergency escape route for the Brittain Colliery. The area around it is now part of Brittain Pit Farm Park. Ten metres after a right-hand bend climb a stile on the left to walk downhill through Jubilee Wood. Climb a stile on the edge of the wood and walk along the left-hand edge of a field to reach a surfaced lane.

4 Turn left and then turn right in a few metres between farm buildings. At a junction of tracks maintain direction for 40m and then bear to the right onto a track which is wire fenced on both sides and initially is paved. This track bends to the left in several hundred metres. Forty metres after the bend climb a stile on the right to follow the left-hand edge of a field. Pass through a gap at the end of the field and bear to the left to a junction of paths in a few metres. Here bear left again to walk with Codnor Park Industrial Estate on the right. At a T-junction at the end of the industrial estate turn right to walk downhill with woodland on the left and the industrial estate on the right to reach a road. Turn left and then right at a T-junction to walk towards Codnor and its Market Place.

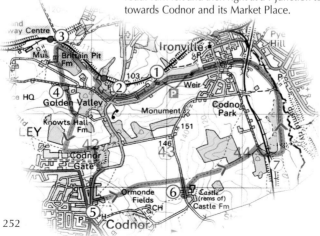

5 Fifty metres before reaching the Red Admiral in Codnor turn left by a public footpath signpost. Follow the track to a stile. Climb the stile and walk along the left-hand edge of a field. At the junction of paths at the end of the field keep ahead with a hedge on the left along the edge of a golf course. Climb a stile to leave the golf course and follow the left-hand edge of two fields to reach a lane.

6 Turn right onto the lane and pass a white house on the left. At a junction of lanes climb a stile on the left in the hedge. Head half right across a field over the top of a ridge, then make for a hedge corner. The ruins of Codnor Castle are on the right. Turn right to walk with a hedge on the right in the direction of a corner of Foxhole Plantation. Climb a stile to join a path which runs along the edge of the plantation. At the end of the plantation climb a stile and walk along the left-hand edge of a field and then keep ahead along the edge of a wood. Ignore the fork a few metres into the wood but at a crossroad of paths with a stile on the left turn right into the wood. At a junction of paths bear to the left to cross a footbridge over a railway line in 20m.

7 Follow the path to a T-junction and turn left. The path winds through the woods to a footbridge over the Cromford Canal. Walk across the footbridge and bear to the left onto the canal towpath. Follow the towpath for several kilometres, passing first Jacksdale on the right and then Ironville, where the old Pinxton Arm joins the Cromford Canal, under a railway and then across a road back to Codnor Park Reservoir.

Refreshments:	Newlands Inn and pubs in Codnor
Toilets:	None
Key Features:	A section of the Cromford Canal; the Midland Railway Centre (01773 747674); Codnor Castle

WALK 53
Tissington and High Peak Trails

After the closure of the Cromford and High Peak Railway in 1967 the track bed from High Peak Junction to Dowlow near Buxton was converted by Derbyshire County Council and the Peak National Park Authority into the 28km/17½ mile High Peak Trail. For information on the Tissington Trail see Walk 21.

Hartington Old Signal Box

Distance:	11.5km/7 miles
Start:	Hartington Old Signal Box on Tissington Trail off the B5054 near Hartington, or the Friden car park on High Peak Trail
Map:	OS Explorer OL24 The Peak District White Peak Area
Terrain:	An easy trail and track walk

ROUTE INSTRUCTIONS

1 Walk back to the entrance to the car park and down a lane to reach the B5054. Turn right onto the road and in 200m bear left onto a walled track which leads to the A515. The route continues straight ahead on the track at the other side of this busy main road but the Jug and Glass Inn is 100m to the right. The track reaches the High Peak Trail in 300m.

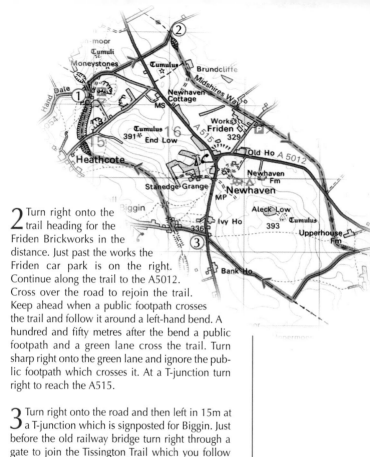

2 Turn right onto the trail heading for the Friden Brickworks in the distance. Just past the works the Friden car park is on the right. Continue along the trail to the A5012. Cross over the road to rejoin the trail. Keep ahead when a public footpath crosses the trail and follow it around a left-hand bend. A hundred and fifty metres after the bend a public footpath and a green lane cross the trail. Turn sharp right onto the green lane and ignore the public footpath which crosses it. At a T-junction turn right to reach the A515.

3 Turn right onto the road and then left in 15m at a T-junction which is signposted for Biggin. Just before the old railway bridge turn right through a gate to join the Tissington Trail which you follow for several kilometres to Hartington Old Signal Box.

Refreshments:	Hartington Old Signal Box and the Jug and Glass Inn on the A515
Toilets:	Hartington Old Signal Box
Key Features:	Sections of the Tissington and High Peak trails and the information centre at Hartington Old Signal Box

Caudwell's Mill, which is operated by the Caudwell's Mill Trust, was opened to the public in 1981 and is the only complete Victorian water-powered roller mill in England. The trust has restored much of the building, which displays the history of the mill and of milling in general, and houses various craft shops. Flour that is periodically produced at the mill is on sale at the premises.

Distance:	9km/5½ miles
Start:	Roadside parking on Woodhouse Lane which is opposite the Peacock Hotel on the A6 at Rowsley. Caudwell's Mill car park off Woodhouse Lane is for patrons only.
Map:	OS Explorer OL24 The Peak District White Peak Area
Terrain:	A gradual climb from Rowsley up onto Stanton Moor and then a descent back off the moor on the return leg

There has been a mill on the River Wye near its confluence with the Derwent at Rowsley for at least 600 years, although we can only be sure of what type of mill from around 1590. At that time there was a corn and walk (fulling) mill, and these were later to be used as a sawmill and a bakery. In 1874 John Caudwell took a lease from the Duke of Rutland and demolished the two now derelict mills and built in their place a large flour and provender (animal food) mill powered by two breast shot wheels. John equipped his Rowsley Mill with the very latest technology, which enabled it to thrive. A few years later, when roller milling replaced stone milling around 1885, Caudwell re-equipped the mill with this new system which enabled him to produce white bread flour quicker and in larger quantities. In 1887 the waterwheel was changed for a water turbine.

In 1887 Caudwell leased the mill to his four sons, who ran it as a partnership in conjunction with their

Caudwell's Mill

other mill at Mansfield until 1899, when the partnership was dissolved and Edward, one of John's sons, took over the mill. Like his father, Edward kept up with the latest innovations in milling practices and continued to make significant capital investments in modernising the mill, and it continued to grow until Edward's death in 1941. His son Edward also kept the business in the family by passing it to his son Sandy Caudwell. The mill closed as a commercial family business in 1978, when it claimed to be the smallest commercial flour millers in the country.

Stanton Moor is a Scheduled Ancient Monument set on a gritstone plateau on the side of the Derwent Valley, which was inhabited during the Bronze Age. Stanton Moor, where cultivated crops, huts and burial mounds were once intermingled, now represents one of the richest archaeological sites in Derbyshire containing numerous prehistoric remains, including over 70 burial mounds, standing stones and a stone circle. Part of the moor is now under the protection of the National Trust.

Nine Ladies Stone Circle is the major prehistoric site on the moor, consisting of nine upright stones set in an

Nine Ladies Stone Circle – Stanton Moor

embanked circle in a sheltered birch wood clearing. There is also a single standing stone nearby known as the King Stone which is thought to be associated with the stone circle.

The Grey Tower, a prominent local landmark, was erected in 1832 by the Thornhills at nearby Stanton Hall to commemorate the passing of the First Reform Act, which came as the result of a long battle and effectively opened the door for parliamentary democracy as we know it today. Earl Grey was the Liberal prime minister who brought about this historic event and the square gritstone tower was strategically placed so that it was in full view of the Duke of Devonshire and Duke of Rutland, both of whom had opposed the bill.

ROUTE INSTRUCTIONS

1 Walk down Woodhouse Lane away from the Peacock Hotel in Rowsley. Rowsley is an estate village mostly owned by the Duke of Rutland whose emblem is a peacock. The hotel was built in 1652 as a private house, becoming an inn around

1828. Cross over the River Wye and when the lane bends to the right continue ahead on a surfaced private road which is a public footpath overlooking the Derwent Valley. After passing through Holly Wood turn right at a public footpath sign on the right in 30m. Follow a wall on the left to a large gate. After the gate bear along the track to the right walking between buildings at Stanton Woodhouse Farm. Immediately after the farm enter a field via a large metal gate and follow a track as it bends to the right, climbing uphill with views of Grey Tower. Shortly after walking between two gateposts there is a public footpath sign where you bear to the left away from the track to a gate. Walk along an enclosed path, passing a quarry on the left, to reach a lane.

2 Turn right onto the lane and at a T-junction turn left as signposted for Stanton in Peak. Climb a stile on the left by a public footpath sign and walk across the middle of a field to enter woodland. At the fork immediately on entering the trees bear to the right to follow a path close to the edge of the wood. Continue ahead at a stile on the right at the edge of Stanton Moor and pass the Grey Tower. Before a large boulder turn right at a T-junction to continue along the edge of the moor with a wire fence on the right and views of Riber Castle.

3 Eventually on reaching a National Trust sign climb a stile on the right to enter the moor. Turn left and then turn right at the junction immediately in front of you to walk past rhododendrons. At a T-junction turn left and then turn right

at a crossroad of paths as signposted for Nine Ladies Stone. Follow this path across the moor, ignoring any offshoots, passing the stone circle on the left and climb a stile at the side of the gate to leave the moor. Maintain direction through several gates to a road.

4 Turn left and just after passing through trees and before entering Stanton in Peak turn right at a public footpath sign onto a private road. Pass a cricket ground to enter woodland and emerge out onto a road. Turn right onto the road with views over the Wye Valley of Haddon Hall and Bakewell. In 100m turn left at a public footpath sign and walk downhill and between two gateposts. Walk next to a line of trees and in a corner of the field pass through a gap and follow the right-hand edge of the next field to a lane.

5 Turn left onto the lane and follow it as it bends first sharply to the left then to the right and back to the left again. On this third bend turn right at a public footpath sign. In 20m pass through a squeeze stile into a field and follow the clear path across a stream. In 10m pass through a gate into a field and walk along a grassy path with the River Wye over to the left. At a large tree bear left onto a track to meet the goit by a lane. Goit is an old Derbyshire term for a man-made watercourse. Turn left onto the lane and follow it around a left-hand bend back to the starting point.

Refreshments:	Pubs at Rowsley and cafe at Caudwell's Mill
Toilets:	Caudwell's Mill
Key Features:	Caudwell's Mill (01629 734374) and Stanton Moor including the Nine Ladies Stone Circle

WALK 55
Upper Longdendale Valley

Distance:	11.5km/7 miles
Start:	Torside Information Centre on the B6105 next to Torside Reservoir
Map:	OS Explorer OL1 The Peak District Dark Peak Area
Terrain:	Easy trail walking surrounded by high hills

The first water from the Upper Longdendale Valley was supplied in 1851, and when the scheme was finally completed in 1877 it formed the largest artificial expanse of water in the world at that time. Today it acts as North West Water's fifth largest resource, connecting to the water supply network for Manchester. The upper three reservoirs (Woodhead, Torside and Rhodeswood) are the supply reservoirs, whilst Valehouse and Bottoms are compensation reservoirs which also release water back to the River Etherow to maintain flows downstream.

The Longdendale Valley has provided a route across the Pennines since the Middle Ages when salt was carried by packhorse. In 1731 a turnpike from Cheshire to Yorkshire was authorised, so the level of trade increased. In the following decades the River Etherow was exploited to provide water for mills. Cotton was made at Vale House Mill, Bottom Lodge Mill and Torside Mill (later a paper mill) and there was also a bleach works at Crowden. Most of these mills were, however, submerged in the reservoirs.

During 1839 to 1845 the first railway link between Manchester and Sheffield was built as part of the Great Central Railway Line. The line incorporated the 5km/ 3 mile long Woodhead Tunnels which were one of the

Upper Longdendale, much of which is a designated a Site of Special Scientific Interest, is a long valley cutting through rugged gritstone moorland in the most easterly section of the River Etherow. The Etherow is one of the South Pennine tributaries of the Mersey. The land ranges from a height of 152m/500ft on the valley floor to over 579m/1900ft at Black Hill in the north and 610m/2000ft at Bleaklow in the south. A 9.5km/ 6 mile chain of five main reservoirs impound the River Etherow through the Upper Longdendale Valley: Bottoms, Valehouse, Rhodeswood, Torside and Woodhead.

Woodhead Chapel

greatest achievements of the formative years of the railway age, though the glowing contemporary tributes to this engineering feat masked the appalling conditions the navvies faced, which cost at least 60 of them their lives and injured hundreds more. Some of the graves of the men who died can be seen at the tiny Woodhead Chapel.

The passenger service on the railway was withdrawn in 1970 and the line finally closed in 1981. The disused trackbed was then purchased by North West Water in 1989 and, in conjunction with the Peak District National Park, it was converted into the 14.5km/9 mile Longdendale Trail in 1992. This trail, which runs from Hadfield Station to the Woodhead Tunnels and then up over the moorland to Windle Edge, now forms part of the Trans-Pennine Trail.

ROUTE INSTRUCTIONS

1 Walk to the back of the car park on the opposite side to the information centre and pass to the side of a large black gate. In 75m turn left onto the Longdendale Trail with Torside Reservoir over to the left. After passing the Old Mill on the right and before the B6105 bends to the left between Torside and the Woodhead Reservoir turn left at a public footpath sign for Crowden. Woodhead Chapel is perched on the hillside opposite. Cross over the B6105 to join the Torside concessionary footpath.

After walking over a footbridge turn left to drop down some steep steps to the side of the reservoir.

2 Follow the clear path to the dam wall and maintain direction along Rhodeswood Reservoir (to shorten the walk cross the dam wall and join the Longdendale Trail) at the end of Rhodeswood Reservoir. Otherwise follow the edge of Valehouse Reservoir and cross the dam wall and turn left into a small parking area.

3 When the track forks keep by the edge of the reservoir and follow it as it later bends to the right and climbs away from the reservoir. Cross over a lane and maintain direction to reach the Longdendale Trail. Turn left back onto the trail and follow it alongside Valehouse and Rhodeswood reservoirs. Walk across the B6105 at Torside Crossing and continue along the trail to where you joined it near Torside Information Centre. Retrace your steps back to the car park.

Refreshments:	Torside Information Centre
Toilets:	Torside Information Centre
Key Features:	The reservoirs of the Upper Longdendale Valley; Woodhead Chapel; Torside Information Centre

WALK 56
Buxton and its Country Park

Distance:	5km/3 miles
Start:	Pavilion Gardens car park off Burlington Road, Buxton town centre or Poole's Cavern and Country Park at Buxton
Map:	OS Explorer OL24 The Peak District White Peak Area
Terrain:	A short walk around the town centre before entering a country park. Climb up to Solomon's Temple on high ground before dropping back down to Buxton.

If you are not familiar with Buxton, and in particular if you approach it from the bleak forbidding hills to its north or west, you will probably be most surprised to be greeted by a town of splendid Georgian to Edwardian buildings, parks and gardens. In the eighteenth and nineteenth centuries Buxton became a fashionable spa town. Its creators attempted to build a resort to rival Bath and Cheltenham, and whilst it never attained this status it was very popular in its own right. At 305m/1000ft Buxton is one of the highest towns in England.

It was the Romans, who had a passion for bathing, who built the first baths at Buxton having discovered warm mineral waters bubbling to the surface, as they do today, at a constant temperature of 28°C/82°F. They called their settlement Aquae Arnemetiae meaning 'the spa of the goddess of the grave'. By 1460 a chapel dedicated to St Anne with a holy well next to it had become well known for its healing properties. Famous visitors include Mary Queen of Scots. In 1535 William Cavendish was appointed by Henry VIII to organise the dissolution of Derbyshire's religious houses. He dissolved the Chapel of St Anne and purchased the land, which was to begin the connection between Buxton and the Cavendish family (later Dukes of Devonshire from Chatsworth House).

'Taking the waters' enjoyed a renaissance in Elizabethan times, though not on the scale witnessed in Georgian and Victorian England when spas became fashionable. In the 1770s Buxton was still very much a market town but the Fifth Duke of Devonshire, impressed by what he had seen at Bath, began to recognise the commercial possibilities of exploiting the thermal and natural springs on his land. Using some of the vast sums of money he had earned from his Ecton copper mine in the Manifold Valley he began an ambitious building programme to attempt to emulate Bath in the Derbyshire hills.

The fifth duke first built during the 1780s the imposing semicircular Crescent, designed by the architect John Carr, known as Carr of York, and modelled on John Wood's Royal Crescent in Bath. The Crescent was the Georgian equivalent of a leisure complex containing three hotels, shops, apartments, coffee and card rooms. A Natural Baths was erected next to it on the site of the Roman version – the baths now house the tourist information centre. Next came the Great Stables built between 1785 and 1790, the Hall Bank and The Square. Opposite The Crescent is an open area called The Slopes which was originally laid out by Sir Jeffrey Wyatville but later modified by Joseph Paxton in about 1840. At the top of The Slopes is the Town Hall built in 1889. At the bottom of The Slopes you pass the Pump Room where visitors took the thermal waters until 1981. Next to it is St Anne's Well, a public pump providing water at a constant 28° C. At the far end of The Slopes, Hall Bank runs off to the left with its elegant line of town houses dating from the 1790s.

Devonshire Royal Hospital, Buxton

265

It was the sixth and seventh dukes who went on to develop Buxton into a fully fledged spa resort. By 1847 the Cavendish family owned 75 per cent of the town. The Great Stables were converted in 1859 to the Devonshire Hospital and in 1881–2 the hospital was covered with a dome which at the time was the largest unsuspended dome in the world (48m/156ft in diameter and weighing 560 tons). More hotels and guesthouses sprung up and the railways arrived, providing access for the popular masses. In 1871 the Pavilion Gardens were laid out on the banks of the River Wye and in 1905 the Opera House opened, which today plays host to the annual international Buxton Festival of Music and the Arts. Bottled Buxton mineral water remains very popular.

The outskirts of Buxton have witnessed centuries of quarrying and lime burning. In the early nineteenth century the Duke of Devonshire planted Grin Low Woods on Grin Low Hill, now a Site of Special Scientific Interest, to hide a waste tip that had accumulated as a byproduct of the industrial use of the land. This was an early and successful example of land reclamation and the area is now a country park containing two other noteworthy features. First, the spectacular natural Poole's Cavern features impressive stalagmites and stalactites, including the world's only known poached egg stalagmites and the longest stalactite in Derbyshire. Poole was a legendary medieval outlaw who allegedly used the cavern as a hide-out. Second, at the top of the 439m/1440ft Grin Low Hill stands Grin Low Tower, or Solomon's Temple. A local industrialist, Solomon Mycock, built this folly to occupy the local unemployed labour and to leave as his own memorial in the late nineteenth century. The 7.5m/25ft mock classical temple is built on top of an Iron Age burial mound and provides a fine viewpoint.

ROUTE INSTRUCTIONS

1 From the car park walk into the Pavilion Gardens, passing the spa swimming pool and

the Pavilion complex. The 23 acre gardens were laid out in 1871 by Edward Milner, a pupil of Sir Joseph Paxton. On reaching a road turn left to pass the front of the Opera House and walk along Water Street. The Devonshire Royal Hospital and the Palace Hotel can be seen ahead. Turn right at the T-junction and keep ahead at George Street. Bear to the right at the roundabout onto The Quadrant and then turn right opposite the Grove Hotel onto The Crescent by Turner's Memorial. At the fork ignore Hartington Road on the left and keep ahead on the pedestrianised Broadwalk, which runs next to the Pavilion Gardens. Joseph Paxton designed this street of fine Victorian houses in the 1860s.

2 Maintain direction for a short distance at the end of the Broadwalk to a junction of roads and cross over onto College Road. In 15m turn right onto Temple Road. Turn left at a T-junction, which is still Temple Road, and at the next T-junction cross over into the car park for Poole's Cavern and Country Park. Take the steps at the back of the car park signposted for Grinlow and Solomon's Temple. At a large crossroad of paths turn left for Solomon's Temple and gently ascend through Grin Woods on a wide clear path. Ignore any offshoots to reach a stile at the top of the woods. Climb the stile for a view of Solomon's Temple over to the left, which you head for.

3 After carefully climbing the folly for an excellent 360-degree viewpoint turn left to head downhill towards Buxton. Pass through a gap in 75m and walk downhill towards the woods but ignore the path by a white sign slightly over to the right. Enter the woods and at the fork immediately in front of you bear to the right. Follow this downhill path to a gap at the edge of the wood which

267

Solomon's Temple

leads onto a playing field. After the gap at the fork walk by a wall on the left down to a marker post. Cross the playing fields and negotiate another gap. Turn left to reach a road junction. Cross over and walk down College Road to a junction you were at earlier close to the end of the Broadwalk. Make for the Broadwalk by crossing Macclesfield Road to join Bath Road. A few metres along the Broadwalk bear left into the Pavilion Gardens. At the fork by the lake keep right and bear right at the end of the lake under a walkway. Maintain direction to a bridge virtually opposite the Pavilion. Cross the bridge and bear to the left to another bridge and return to the starting point.

Refreshments:	Pubs and cafes in Buxton
Toilets:	Buxton
Key Features:	The former spa town of Buxton; Poole's Cavern and Country Park; the views from the Victorian folly Solomon's Temple

WALK 57
Matlock and Matlock Bath

Distance:	8km/5 miles
Start:	Car park at Matlock Bath Railway Station. Alternative starting points in Matlock Bath are the car park at the Pavilion (Lead Mining Museum/tourist information office) or the car park on Temple Road, Matlock Bath. The long-stay car park at Matlock could also be used.
Map:	OS Explorer OL24 The Peak District White Peak Area
Terrain:	Two very steep climbs out of Matlock Bath in quick succession

Matlock and Matlock Bath, both tourist honeypots, are set a few kilometres apart on the banks of the River Derwent, providing an un-believable number of attractions in spec-tacular surroundings. The Masson Hill area has become part of a tourist complex called the Heights of Abraham which can either be accessed on foot, if you don't mind a steep climb, or in a more leisurely manner from the cablecar station passed near the end of this walk.

Matlock is a busy little town once noted for its hydros (temples of healing by water) such as the one built by John Smedley from Riber Castle, which is now Derbyshire's County Hall. The evocative ruins of Riber Castle, a mock medieval fairytale castle, sit on top of a hill overlooking Matlock. The property was designed and built by John Smedley, a local wealthy textile manufac-turer. Constructed from local gritstone, it was completed in 1862 at a cost of £60,000. Smedley died in 1874 but his widow continued to live at Riber until 1888. It then became a boy's school until 1930. The castle stood empty until 1936 when the council purchased it at auc-tion for £1965. During the Second World War Riber was requisitioned and used as an emergency food supplies depot before being handed back to the council in 1948. It was left derelict and all that remains is a roofless shell.

Matlock Bath lies downstream in a dramatic lime-stone gorge between the 91m/300ft towering crag of High Tor on one side and Masson Hill on the other.

During the late seventeenth century the waters in the area gradually gained a reputation for their medicinal properties. In 1698 the Old Bath Hotel opened and during the course of the next century Matlock Bath became a fashionable village for the very well-to-do, who built grand villas on the lower slopes of Masson Hill. At this time the growth of Matlock Bath was constrained by its relatively poor transport communications as there was only one road in and this was a dead end. Later a road was also opened up from Cromford. Matlock Bath reached its height during the Regency period when it became a favourite holiday retreat for the middle classes as transport links improved and the village became a spa resort with an interesting blend of architectural styles. The main reason people came to Matlock Bath was for the 'waters' but there were other attractions, not least the spectacular setting and surrounding scenery. The air was said to be very healthy, and the caves, along with other natural phenomena and the Pleasure Gardens, all helped provide the complete holiday. The spa received many famous visitors including Byron, Ruskin and even a young Victoria before she became Queen. It was the building of a railway through the spa that encouraged the crowds and began a decline as the 'quality' moved out and commercialism moved in.

The southern face of Masson Hill is known as the Heights of Abraham after a likeness was noted between the gorge here and the St Lawrence Gorge in Quebec, site of a famous battle in 1759. Lead mining has taken place on Masson Hill possibly as far back as Roman times. Rutland Cavern and the Great Masson Cavern, both part natural cave and part lead mine, were opened up as show caves in 1821 and 1844 respectively. Close to these caverns the Victoria Prospect Tower was built as a prominent landmark and superb viewpoint, and the Pleasure Gardens were developed with exotic trees and shrubs.

High Tor on the opposite side of the gorge to the Heights of Abraham was also once a Victorian Pleasure Ground and is now maintained as a park by the council.

Gulliver's Kingdom, a more recent addition to Matlock Bath on Masson Hill, is a theme park for families with young children which opened in 1978. The Derwent Gardens provide another example of Victorian gardens by the River Derwent. Every year from late August to the end of October this stretch of the riverbank is decorated with illuminations, which provide a thrilling background for the town's Venetian Nights, when illuminated water pageants take place on the river.

The Pavilion next to the River Derwent now houses a large information centre and the Lead Mining Museum. In the days when Matlock Bath was a spa this building contained the pump room and is typical of 1880s spa architecture. The Lead Mining Museum was opened in 1978 and traces the history of lead mining in Derbyshire from the Roman era to fairly recent times. It is owned by the Peak District Mines Historical Society which also owns the Temple Mine on Temple Road (this can be included as part of your visit to the Lead Mining Museum). The Society also owns the Magpie Lead Mine near Sheldon (see Walk 29).

Also on Temple Road is a model railway which has been handmade in intricate detail and consists of a series of reconstructions of the Midland Railway Company's track through some of the most scenic parts of the Peak District. The Whistlestop Countryside Centre can be found in a section of the Victorian railway station buildings and provides an information and education facility run by Derbyshire Wildlife Trust.

ROUTE INSTRUCTIONS

1 Walk through the car park away from the railway station, and towards the back of the car park look out for a footpath signpost on the right for 'Lovers Walk'. In a few metres at the fork bear to the right on the main path. This park was known to be in existence prior to 1742, making it one of the oldest riverside parks in England. Many of the paths are of ancient origin and have been used by

local lead miners for centuries. At a fork just after passing an information board bear left onto the higher path to climb steps. Ignore the next two off-shoots, climbing up to a view of Gulliver's Kingdom on the other side of the gorge. The path now follows a wooden fence on the left along the top of the hill. Later the main path bears to the right into the woodland and you begin to descend to the River Derwent. The path winds down to a junction of paths by an old ruined building. Here turn right and continue to wind down through the woodland to the riverside.

2 Turn right and then cross over a footbridge in 75m. This footbridge is not shown on the OS map. Turn right at the end of the footbridge as sign-posted for 'Tourist Information' to walk through the Derwent Gardens and pass through an ornate blue gate at the far end to soon reach the A6. If you turn right here you will reach the Pavilion containing the tourist information office and Lead Mining Museum in 20m. To follow the route of the walk turn left at this point and cross the A6 with extreme care. Turn right onto Temple Road in 20m. Pass the entrance on the left for Gulliver's Kingdom and then just before the entrance for the Temple Mine turn left by a public footpath signpost for Upperwood. Climb a few steps onto the entrance road to Gulliver's Kingdom

but turn right in 15m onto a path which climbs steeply up by the side of the theme park. At a fork bear left to continue the ascent to a lane.

3 Turn right onto the lane and when it starts to drop downhill and curve to the right look out for a path by a yellow waymarker on the left. This marks the start of another very steep climb along the edge of a wood. Ignore any offshoots until you reach a signpost at the top of the hill. Turn right at this point for Matlock and walk through wood-land. Close to the edge of the wood at a fork bear to the right and cross over a lane which leads into the Heights of Abraham, although there is no pub-lic access at this point. In a few metres climb a stile by a marker post and walk half right to another marker post in 20m to join a grassy downhill path. Shortly on reaching the next marker post at a junc-tion of paths bear to the right to climb a stile at the side of a gate. Follow the path to another stile at the side of a gate and then keep to the left-hand edge of a field by a wall. At the end of the field bear to the left to walk with a fence on the right to reach a stile at the side of Masson Farm. Twenty metres after the stile there is a public footpath sign-post for Matlock Dale and you walk with a high wall on the right to reach St John's Road. Turn left onto the lane to reach the A6 after passing the unusual St John's Chapel.

4 Turn left onto the A6 and follow it into Matlock. Cross Matlock Bridge over the River Derwent and then just before a roundabout cross over the road using a pedestrian crossing and enter Hall Leys Park. Follow a broad surfaced path close to the river and keep ahead at a footbridge. Opposite a house with a very ornate lamp post turn right over a bridge and right again at a T-junc-tion in 20m. Walk along a surfaced path with high cliffs on the left and pass under a railway bridge.

When you are opposite a footbridge across the river turn left under a railway bridge and walk uphill through woodland along a paved path. When you reach the edge of housing turn right by a sign for the grounds of High Tor.

5 The clear path gently climbs up to the summit of High Tor with ever increasing 360-degree views. At a fork close to the summit keep ahead for 15m and then turn right to reach an information board at the summit. There are two paths from the summit and either option can be taken. The right fork is the more interesting of the options but it is not suitable for small children or pets as it follows a vertiginous narrow ledge called Giddy Edge. If you follow Giddy Edge you will reach a T-junction in 100m which meets the alternative route. Turn right to descend through the woodland on the main path winding down to the cablecar station for the Heights of Abraham. Do not walk under the railway bridge after the cablecar station but turn left for Matlock Bath Station and the Whistlestop Countryside Centre on a surfaced path. Cross over the railway line back into the railway station car park. The Whistlestop Countryside Centre is on the right.

Refreshments:	Pubs and cafes in Matlock and Matlock Bath
Toilets:	Matlock and Matlock Bath
Key Features:	The numerous tourist attractions in the area coupled with the excellent setting and views (Heights of Abraham – 01629 582365, Lead Mining Museum – 01629 583834, Gulliver's Kingdom – 01629 585540 and Riber Castle – 01629 582073)

WALK 58
Dovedale

Distance:	11.5km/7 miles or shorter version 8km/5 miles, which is necessary in wet conditions as the stretch along the River Dove from the bottom of Hall Dale to Mill Dale can become impassable on the Raven's Tor side of the river
Start:	The main Dovedale car park past the entrance to the Izaak Walton Hotel
Map:	OS Explorer OL24 The Peak District White Peak Area
Terrain:	A very short but steep climb as you move away from Ilam and a steep and potentially slippery descent down to the River Dove. Also see comments above under 'Distance'.

Dovedale has been famed for its great beauty since Victorian times, and this gem must not be missed as it is arguably the most scenic of the Derbyshire dales.

This very popular valley can become a victim of its own beauty at certain times, as on a sunny and warm Sunday several thousand visitors will flock into the dale, although most stay close to the Stepping Stones at the entrance to the valley. Most of Dovedale is now owned

Stepping Stones, Dovedale

275

by the National Trust which works hard to keep the well-trodden footpaths in good condition. An added dimension to the landscape, along with the delightful winding river, is a number of prominent rock formations and caverns which have formed in this limestone gorge, all of which have been named and are easily identifiable.

ROUTE INSTRUCTIONS

1 From the car park entrance cross over the road and climb a stile onto a track. In 20m bear to the right up some steps to a stile. Head across a field passing the Izaak Walton Hotel on the left. After the next two stiles there is a fork of paths. Keep to the left as signposted for 'Ilam' across two fields to a stile by the side of a gate and onto a track. At a junction of paths just before Ilam turn right for Stanshope so that you are walking uphill with a wall on the left.

2 Pass a pond and continue by a wall with Bunster Hill to your right. The path then moves away from the wall to reach a stile. Do not climb the stile but turn right in front of it with a wall on the left to climb very steeply uphill. When the path bends to the right climb a stile in a wall corner into a field. There is no path on the ground in this field but you head for a large solitary tree on the brow of the hill and pass through a metal gate to the right of the tree. Walk half left over to another metal

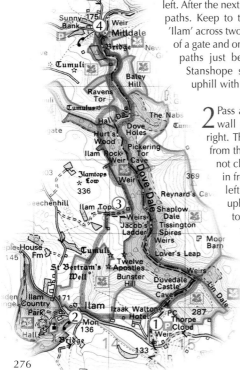

276

gate just before a barn onto a track lined with trees. At a T-junction turn right away from Ilam Tops Farm.

Dove Holes, Dovedale

3 Walk over a cattle grid just before Air Cottage and pass through a small gate on the right in 20m and bear left to a stile in 15m. After the stile the path bears to the left along the top of a ridge around Air Cottage to reach a track. Turn right onto the track and climb a ladder stile 10m to the right of a gate. Then climb another ladder stile on the right into Dovedale Wood. At the junction of paths in front of you turn to the left to walk along the

edge of the wood. Keep ahead at a marker post for Dovedale. When you can see a stile over to the left the path then bends sharply to the right and starts the steep winding descent into Dovedale to eventually reach the river. In wet weather the shorter version of the walk will need to be followed from here by turning right and crossing the river by a footbridge and turning right again. Otherwise turn left and follow the path which runs close to the river and soon passes Dove Holes and then later by a series of stiles moves slightly away from the river to reach Milldale.

4 Turn right on reaching Milldale to pass the National Trust Information Centre and cross over Viator Bridge to join the magnificent path through Dovedale. Once more you pass Dove Holes to reach a footbridge with Ilam Rock on the right and Pickering Tor on the left. Further up the river is Lions Head Rock and Reynards Cave followed by Dovedale Church, Tissington Spires, Lovers Leap, Twelve Apostles and Dovedale Castle before reaching the Stepping Stones beneath the vantage point of Thorpe Cloud. The river can be crossed at this point and you then turn left or, if you prefer, several hundred metres further along the river a footbridge makes an easier crossing. If the latter option is taken turn left after the footbridge to return to the starting point.

Refreshments:	Dovedale car park, the Izaac Walton Hotel and a cafe at Milldale
Toilets:	Dovedale car park and Milldale car park
Key Features:	Dovedale and its rock formations

WALK 59
Derwent Dams

Distance:	12km/7½ miles
Start:	Fairholmes car park between the Derwent Reservoir and the Ladybower
Map:	OS Explorer OL1 The Peak District Dark Peak Area
Terrain:	Other than a steep climb away from the Derwent Reservoir up onto moorland this is not a difficult walk. It is mainly, however, across moorland and should be saved for fine weather.

Howden was the first of the Derwent Dams to be built (from 1901 to 1912) and the Derwent was started a year later in 1902 and completed in 1916. Conifers were planted to stabilise the ground and reduce the amount of soil washed into the reservoirs. Today it is recognised that this was perhaps not the best plan and the surrounding forestry is being carefully managed over time. Close to the edge of the Derwent Reservoir a temporary 'tin

To satisfy the needs of growing industrial towns such as Sheffield, Nottingham, Derby and Leicester a chain of reservoirs was built in the Upper Derwent Valley close to the source of the River Derwent on Howden Moor. This deep and narrow gritstone valley, coupled with the high rainfall off the surrounding moorland, made this an ideal location for creating reservoirs. Today this has left an artificial but attractive landscape which draws high visitor numbers for leisure purposes and is the subject of an award-winning traffic and visitor management scheme. It also, under the control of Severn Trent Water, still provides a water supply to Sheffield and the East Midlands.

Ladybower Reservoir and Ashopton Viaduct

town' was built at Birchinlee to house the navvies and their families. The nickname 'tin town' was derived from the structure of the corrugated iron huts which were all demolished 15 years later. A railway line to provide transport access was built in the construction phase along much of what today is the road between Ashopton Viaduct and Fairholmes car park.

Between 1935 and 1944 the water supply was added to by construction of the Ladybower Reservoir which was officially opened in 1945 by George VI. During the Second World War RAF 617 Squadron used the reservoirs for low-level practice to prepare for a raid in 1943 on key German dams. The film Dam Busters also used the Derwent Dams as a location. The construction of the Howden and Derwent resulted in the sacrifice of very few buildings, but the Ladybower eventually necessitated the demolition of two small villages, Ashopton and Derwent. Ashopton lies near the Ashopton Viaduct and there is very little chance of the water level being low enough to view the ruins. The site of the village of Derwent is passed on this walk and there are still a few signs of the tiny village that grew around Derwent Hall, built in 1672, depending on the level of the water. The only structure to 'survive' the submerging of the villages is the Derwent packhorse bridge which was dismantled and rebuilt at the far end of the Howden reservoirs at Slippery Stones.

ROUTE INSTRUCTIONS

1 Take the public footpath next to the information centre and turn right onto a lane in 50m with the dam wall of the Derwent on your left. When the lane bends to the right at the end of the dam wall turn left but ignore the gate and take the higher forestry path. Pass the edge of the dam wall and climb a stile onto a rough track which runs beside the edge of the reservoir. Cross over a bridge and then when the reservoir bends gently to the left in a more open area turn right at a public footpath sign for Bradfield and Strines.

2 Walk uphill through woodland and cross a stream by a wall. After emerging from the trees continue heading uphill on the clear winding path up Walkers Clough entering National Trust land. At a crossroads by a public footpath sign continue ahead and at a T-junction bear to the right to reach a stile by a public footpath sign for Strines. Climb the stile and continue ahead. At a junction bear left and then at a grassy fork keep left. The path bends to the right at the bottom of a hill before beginning a short ascent of Lost Lad. At a T-junction maintain direction, climbing steps to reach the summit.

3 This delightful stretch along Derwent Edge, the most northerly of the gritstone edges, has now been slabbed for erosion control. The route drops

down and rises back up onto Black Tor. Pass the trig point over to the left and then turn right at a junction of paths along the edge with a number of unusual rock formations to guide the way. First you pass the Cakes of Bread on the left, then the Dove Stone at Dovestone Tor. Next is the Salt Cellar on the right which leads on to White Tor, and the grand finale is the Wheel Stones, sometimes also called the Coach and Horses. Several hundred metres after the Wheel Stones turn right at a crossroad of paths by a public footpath sign to leave the edge and begin the descent to the Ladybower Reservoir.

4 Follow the path down to a junction with a track by a wall. Turn right onto the track for 30m and then turn left through a gate by a public footpath sign for 'Derwent'. Continue downhill towards a plantation. Pass through a gate at the edge of the plantation to walk with the plantation on the left. Pass through another gate at the far side of the plantation to walk with a wall on the left. Shortly after the next gate cross over a stream and walk between farm buildings. After the buildings continue initially with a wall on the right and then a wire fence. The path bends to the right with good views of the reservoir up to the Ashopton Viaduct to a gate onto a track which runs beside the reservoir. Turn right onto the track and take some time to read the information board on the lost village of the Derwent before crossing a bridge over Mill Brook. Follow the track which becomes a surfaced lane and bends to the left by the Derwent dam wall. From this point retrace your steps to the starting point.

Refreshments:	Fairholmes car park
Toilets:	Fairholmes car park
Key Features:	Derwent Dams; Derwent Edge; the information centre at Fairholmes car park (01433 650953)

WALK 60
Carsington Water

Distance:	13km/8 miles
Start:	Carsington Water Visitor Centre off the B5035 between Wirksworth and Kniveton. Alternative starting points are the car parks at Millfields or the Sheepwash car park.
Map:	OS Explorer OL24 The Peak District White Peak Area
Terrain:	Easy lakeside walking, although gently undulating in parts

The award-winning Carsington Water Visitor Centre, owned by Severn Trent Water, attracts a million visitors a year and follows the journey of water from the reservoir to the tap through interactive displays. The centre houses a Kugel (German for ball), a water feature consisting of a one-ton ball of Bavarian granite which can be rotated in the water at the slightest touch.

Carsington Water is the ninth largest reservoir in England and was opened in 1992. Most of the Peak District reservoirs gather water from acid moorland so they are low in nutrients, which affects the level of aquatic plant and animal life they can support. Carsington is different in this respect and attracts numerous birds and wildlife.

Carsington Water

Hopton has been the country seat of the Gells, a prominent Derbyshire family, since the fifteenth century, although they have lived in the area since 1208. They built Hopton Hall during Elizabethan times but altered it in the Georgian style during the late eighteenth century. It was only in 1989 that the Gells sold the hall, which still remains a private residence. The family wealth came from the exploitation of the nearby limestone quarries. Phillip Gell was also owner of the Viyella mill at Cromford and was responsible for the construction of the Via Gellia, a road that runs along the valley to the west of Cromford. Sir John Gell was a distinguished parliamentary general in the Civil War. The village itself shares the church at Carsington and includes a number of interesting stone-built cottages.

Carsington consists of a line of attractive cottages, and the Parish Church of St Margaret with Carsington Pastures rising steeply behind. Although its location remains a mystery, many archaeologists believe Carsington to be the site of Lutaderum, the Roman administrative lead centre.

The Kugel at Carsington Water Visitor Centre

This walk follows the yellow waymarked route around the reservoir and through the villages of Hopton and Carsington.

ROUTE INSTRUCTIONS

1 With your back to the entrance to the visitor centre turn left and at the end of the building keep ahead. The path then bends to the left with a parking area on the right. Cross over the entrance road to the sailing club to join the path opposite. Bear to the left by a signpost for 'Millfields'. At the end of the trees the reservoir comes into

full view. Keep ahead at the junction of paths in 40m to continue by the edge of the reservoir towards Millfields.

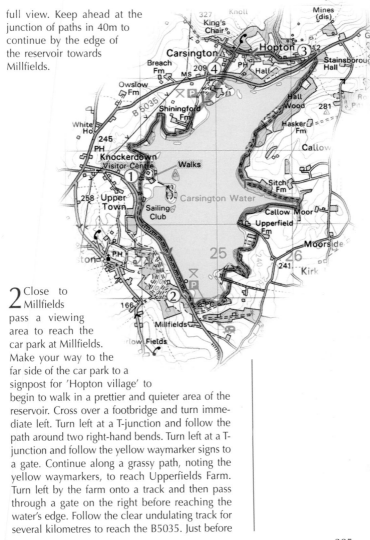

2 Close to Millfields pass a viewing area to reach the car park at Millfields. Make your way to the far side of the car park to a signpost for 'Hopton village' to begin to walk in a prettier and quieter area of the reservoir. Cross over a footbridge and turn immediate left. Turn left at a T-junction and follow the path around two right-hand bends. Turn left at a T-junction and follow the yellow waymarker signs to a gate. Continue along a grassy path, noting the yellow waymarkers, to reach Upperfields Farm. Turn left by the farm onto a track and then pass through a gate on the right before reaching the water's edge. Follow the clear undulating track for several kilometres to reach the B5035. Just before reaching the road there is a good view of Hopton Hall which cannot be seen from the village itself as it is hidden behind high walls.

3 Cross over the road with care to the track opposite by a signpost for Hopton village. Turn left onto the lane through Hopton and keep ahead at a T-junction to reach Carsington, passing its church and the Miners Arms. Turn left at the village green and then left again in a few metres. Turn right onto a track opposite the back of the Miners Arms and when this track bends to the right keep ahead. Climb a stile at the side of a gate to reach the B5035 which you cross back over again to the path on the other side.

4 At the fork in front of you keep to the left and ignore all offshoots to reach the Sheepwash car park. Cross over the entrance road to the car park and again maintain direction when meeting this roadway at the opposite end of the car park. Keep ahead at a crossroads and follow the path around to the right. Along this stretch the route leaves the main track several times by the yellow waymarkers and then soon rejoins it to return to the visitor centre.

Refreshments:	Carsington Water Visitor Centre, Millfields and a pub in Carsington village
Toilets:	Carsington Water Visitor Centre and Millfields
Key Features:	Carsington Water and its large visitor centre complex (01629 540696), and the villages of Hopton and Carsington

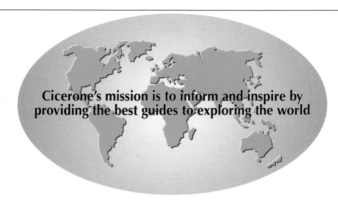

Cicerone's mission is to inform and inspire by providing the best guides to exploring the world

Since its foundation over 30 years ago, Cicerone has specialised in publishing guidebooks and has built a reputation for quality and reliability. It now publishes nearly 300 guides to the major destinations for outdoor enthusiasts, including Europe, UK and the rest of the world.

Written by leading and committed specialists, Cicerone guides are recognised as the most authoritative. They are full of information, maps and illustrations so that the user can plan and complete a successful and safe trip or expedition – be it a long face climb, a walk over Lakeland fells, an alpine traverse, a Himalayan trek or a ramble in the countryside.

With a thorough introduction to assist planning, clear diagrams, maps and colour photographs to illustrate the terrain and route, and accurate and detailed text, Cicerone guides are designed for ease of use and access to the information.

If the facts on the ground change, or there is any aspect of a guide that you think we can improve, we are always delighted to hear from you.

Cicerone Press
2 Police Square Milnthorpe Cumbria LA7 7PY
Tel:01539 562 069   Fax:01539 563 417
e-mail:info@cicerone.co.uk   web:www.cicerone.co.uk

CICERONE